T0283453

Zero to Rich

Zero to Rich

Secrets to Becoming a Millionaire by 30

Fiona Smith

WILEY

Library of Congress Cataloging-in-Publication Data is Available:

Names: Smith, Fiona (Blogger), author.
Title: Zero to rich : secrets to becoming a millionaire by 30 / Fiona Smith.
Description: First edition. | Hoboken, New Jersey : Wiley, [2024]
Identifiers: LCCN 2023037626 (print) | LCCN 2023037627 (ebook) | ISBN 9781394222612 (cloth) | ISBN 9781394222636 (adobe pdf) | ISBN 9781394222629 (epub)
Subjects: LCSH: Strategic planning. | Risk management. | Finance, Personal. | Success in business. | Wealth.
Classification: LCC HD30.28 .S55875 2024 (print) | LCC HD30.28 (ebook) | DDC 658.4/012—dc23/eng/20231103
LC record available at https://lccn.loc.gov/2023037626
LC ebook record available at https://lccn.loc.gov/2023037627

Cover Design: Paul McCarthy
Cover Art: © Shutterstock|Masson

SKY10063991_010824

Dedicated to my loving, supportive family and my ray of sunshine, Louis.

Contents

Acknowledgments

To my mom and dad. I am so thankful to have you as parents. You are my rock, and I don't know where I would be or what I would do without you both. Through life's many ups and downs, you both have been by my side and I would not be here without your undying love, support, and wise words (although I may not have always listened to them initially!). Thank you for educating me, for sacrificing everything you did for me, and for shaping me into the person I am today.

To Callum, who left behind everything he knew, took a leap of faith in me, encouraged me daily, and blindly stood by my side through thick and thin. Your encouragement, words of wisdom, humor, and reality checks have kept me going. I would never be where I am today without you. You built up my confidence and you are the person I turn to during the tough times. Thank you for your love, understanding, and continuous support.

To my baby, my French bulldog, Louis. Louis, you are my ray of sunshine. You bring happiness, luck, and love everywhere you go. From hearing your snores echoing through the hallway to seeing your funny facial expressions while writing my book. Even if I have a bad day, you infuse it with laughter, cuddles, and love. I don't know what I would do without you. Thank you for holding me together when I'm about to fall apart and for loyally always being by my side.

To my big brother, Finley. You are always there for me and more importantly for my parents. You see the simple things in life – from sparkling sunflecks to the ephemeral buzz of a butterfly – as the magical wonders of the world. Thank you for only seeing the good in us and for showing us how to enjoy life's daily treasures. Don't ever change the way you are.

To my mentor, who took me under his wing and taught me invaluable lessons about entrepreneurship, mindset, and winning. You saw me as a kid who was hungry to learn, hungry to grow in life, and hungry to leave a lasting impact. You encouraged me along the way – to embrace those difficult choices and to never fear failure. Thank you for helping me believe in myself to make the right choices, especially when there is a fork in the road.

To Kevin, Stacey, Shannon, and everyone else at the Wiley Crew who was there every step of the way. I'm honored to be a part of your team; thank you for believing in me, and for helping me write my story.

And finally, to everyone else who has been a part of my journey: it really does take a village and I want to sincerely thank everyone who has stood by me, who has mentored me, helped me grow, and encouraged me to pursue my dreams.

About the Author

Author | Entrepreneur | Personal Finance Ninja | *Forbes* Contributor | Dog Lover

Hey, friends!

I'm Fiona Smith (aka The Millennial Money Woman). My purpose is to help you find your path to financial freedom.

My journey started back when I was about 10 years old, when I witnessed my grandparents, who had worked extremely hard all their lives and were about to retire, lose every cent they saved due to poor financial planning.

Although I didn't know exactly what this event meant for me or my future, all I knew was that I would try my best to help others – and my family – avoid going through the same financial difficulties my family once did.

After earning my Master's Degree in Personal Financial Planning, working as a wealth advisor for seven years, advising 453 millionaires on how to build wealth, and after going through the turbulent times of COVID-19, I knew it was time for me to start my personal finance platform, *The Millennial Money Woman*.

Three years and counting, The Millennial Money Woman could not have achieved the following without your help:

Gained 230k+ followers on Twitter.

Listed as a Top 500 Entrepreneur of 2023.

Gained over 2.5k YouTube subscribers in just two months.

Featured articles on *Forbes*, Benzinga, Experian, MSN, and others.

Featured as a speaker at an international event with 1,000+ attendees.

So thank YOU for your continuous support.

While this world may be cruel and harsh, you are NOT alone.

And that's why I've written this book – dedicated to YOU.

The reader who is dedicated to improving their personal financial situation.

This book and my blog will help break down difficult financial topics into simple and step-by-step guides to help you pursue and realize your financial goals.

Let's get started.

Disclaimer

Before you start diving into this book, please keep in mind that:

- I'm not a financial advisor.
- I don't know your personal financial situation.
- I cannot provide you with customized financial advice.

The lessons in this book are:

- From my knowledge base.
- From my millionaire mentor.
- From my personal experience.

If you are seeking financial advice that is:

- Specific,
- Actionable, and/or
- Customized,

. . . then I would suggest after reading this book you consider researching a local financial professional who can review your financial situation and discuss customized recommendations for your personal scenario.

Here's a tip for when you search for financial professionals:

Consider looking for a Certified Financial Planner® (aka CFP®). Typically speaking, CFP®'s are fiduciaries (which means that by law a CFP® has to do what is in *your* best interest . . . in other words, they should not be selling you financial products where they would earn nice commissions, unless those products genuinely fit into your financial picture).

If you do decide to hire a financial professional, I would also suggest interviewing several professionals *before* you decide to hire them.

The interview meeting (aka introductory meeting) is almost always free, but I would confirm that with your financial professional before you move forward.

Always make sure to do your research *before* hiring a financial professional.

The information within this book should *not* be considered financial advice. Do not rely on the information and advice within this book as an alternative to the advice provided to you by a Certified Public Accountant (CPA), financial advisor, CFP®, or other licensed financial professional.

The goal of this book is simply to provide you with a guide to help you understand some of the steps that you may want to pursue to build wealth.

Before you make any drastic changes to your financial picture, you should consider consulting a financial professional so that you can receive a customized financial plan.

Now that you read my not-so-exciting disclaimer, let's get to it! Enjoy!

Chapter 1

Introduction

Who here feels that learning about money is like learning a different language?

I certainly did.

When I first started learning about money, I honestly thought that the financial professionals wrote everything in secret code.

Seriously.

If you don't have prior financial experience, try tuning in to a professional finance talk show or read a finance college book.

. . . You'll soon see that pretty much *EVERY* sentence will have an abbreviation like:

- RIA.
- IRA.
- IAR.
- ETF.
- EFT.
- 403b.
- 401k.
- DAF.
- QCD.
- RMD.
- IDGT.

What's worse is that many of these abbreviations mean something different if the letters are switched!

Talk about making things complicated!

Oh, and for those of you who are wondering what the preceding terms mean, I created a quick table for you below:

Term	Decoded	In Plain English
RIA	Registered Investment Advisor	Investment firm that advises high-net-worth clients
IRA	Individual Retirement Account	A tax-advantaged retirement account
IAR	Investment Advisor Representative	Investment firm that works for an RIA
ETF	Exchange Traded Fund	Basket of investments in one fund that's traded on the stock exchange
EFT	Electronic Fund Transfer	A way to move funds from one account to another – electronically
403b	N/A	A tax-advantaged retirement plan offered by your employer (which is typically a government or public school employer)
401k	N/A	A tax-advantaged retirement plan offered by your employer (which is often a private employer)
DAF	Donor Advised Fund	A tax-advantaged investment account you can open to contribute money (tax deductible) and later withdraw for qualified charities

Term	Decoded	In Plain English
QCD	Qualified Charitable Distribution	If you are 70.5+ and want to withdraw money from a pre-tax account and don't want to pay taxes on the withdrawal, a QCD is a legal way to avoid paying taxes by donating your withdrawal directly to a qualified charity
RMD	Required Minimum Distribution	The amount of money you have to, by law, withdraw from most retirement accounts when you turn age 72 (per current laws); you will likely have to pay taxes on your RMD
IDGT	Intentionally Defective Grantor Trust	An estate planning strategy to help you save money on estate taxes, among other fees and taxes

If you decided to skip over this big box of terms and definitions, that's totally cool . . . you'll be reading more about them later in the book.

My point is that someone who has not studied finance will likely avoid financial topics since there are so many abbreviations and foreign words . . . and I don't blame them.

It's scary.

And oftentimes, we have *no idea* where to even start learning.

I sure didn't when I started my finance journey.

So Let Me Tell You a Secret

There's one wealth-building formula that is proven.

The formula is this:

Building Wealth = Earning > Spending

That's it.

It's really that simple.

But, not many of us actually stick with this formula – just like many of us don't stick to a regular diet.

To build wealth, you need to spend less than you earn.

Instead, we often spend $100s, if not $1,000s on "get rich quick" schemes just like we spend $100s, if not $1,000s on "lose weight fast" schemes.

When, in reality, you shouldn't have to spend any money. Just like the winning formula to wealth is *earning* > *spending*, the winning formula to losing weight is *caloric burn* > *caloric intake*.

And yet, we simply can't seem to stick to those simple equations – that's just human nature.

Why?

Because we are emotional beings.

If we were Spock (from *Star Trek*), then it would be easy to stick to these logical, non-emotional formulas.

But we're not Spock.

We're human . . . and humans are driven by emotion.

Emotions are the No. 1 reason why we tend to:
- Eat more.
- Go broke.
- Procrastinate.
- Exercise less.
- Spend impulsively.

And because of our emotions, we often have trouble sticking to a single plan.

So, let's get down to the real question.

Fact or Fiction: Is Building Wealth Hard?

Your definition of *wealth* may be completely different from someone else's definition of wealth – and that's perfectly OK.

For the purposes of this book, the definition of *wealth* simply means that you build a net worth where you don't stress about money.

That could mean you build a net worth to support your $20,000 per year lifestyle or that could mean you build a net worth to support your $200,000 per year lifestyle.

So is building wealth hard?

The answer is no.

Technically.

The reason why most people struggle with building wealth is because of:
- Laziness.
- Lack of purpose.
- Analysis paralysis.
- No system in place.

And honestly, I think many people are just too scared to start.

That's why I am writing this book.

To help guide you through the labyrinth of making money.

The very first step if you want to build wealth is to find your purpose (which we discuss in the first chapter of this book).

If you don't have a purpose and have no idea *why* you're actually trying to build wealth . . . then you're probably not going to be very motivated to start your journey.

My purpose to building wealth is:
- My **parents** (I want to retire them early).
- My **family** (I don't want them to stress about money).
- My **future** (I want to have time to do the things I want).

And finally, I think many people struggle building wealth because there is *so* much information in today's world that many of us just stop before even starting.

Think back to that list of abbreviations.

For anyone who is not from the finance world, that list probably looked like a bunch of gobbledygook (aka a different language).

If I listen to the media spouting off abbreviations and terms like the ones I mentioned, I probably would tune out the information too.

I don't blame you.

That's why so many people have trouble starting: There is too much noise.

And that's why I hope this book will help break down money matters for you in plain English manner.

This book's simple goal is to help you get started.

Here's what my book is not:
- Technical.
- Filled with jargon.
- Difficult to understand.
- For advanced investors.

On the contrary, here is what my book is:
- Basic.
- Step-by-step.
- Breaks down finance jargon.
- For beginner to intermediate investors.

This book is designed to motivate you to:
- Pay off debt.
- Start investing.
- Continue investing.
- Think like a millionaire.
- Start on the wealth-building journey.
- Build the future you want, while still having fun.

And ultimately, I'm not here to tell you to stop drinking your $5 Starbucks coffee or to stop indulging in your $15 avocado toasts.

But, I am here to help point you in the right direction, give you the right motivation, and use simple mathematics to discuss why investing today is so important if you want to achieve the goal of building wealth tomorrow.

Ultimately, you'll learn about these key messages:
- Failure is not fatal.
- Become a lazy millionaire.
- Your purpose is your motivation.
- A small leak can sink a big ship – watch out for small, recurring costs.
- To be above average, you'll have to do what the average person won't.

But, the most important message is this:
If you want to make a change in your future, start by laying the foundation today.
In other words, start now.
Stop procrastinating.

After every chapter in this book, I leave you with a few fun follow-up steps that you can take to crush your goals and start your path to building modern wealth.

And most importantly, remember to have fun, enjoy the book, and take notes if you want.

If anything, I hope you remember this:
You don't have to be a professional Wall Street hedge fund manager to win with investing.
Anyone can do it, as long as you start.
Let's dive right in.

Chapter 2

Determine Your Purpose

"So what's your secret?"

I had just ordered a foaming cup of hot coffee at the bakery and seated myself opposite my mentor.

"What secret?" he asked, not expecting my question.

"What's your secret to getting so rich?" I asked, holding my warm cup, leaning into the conversation, in an effort not to miss a single word that my mentor would say.

Enter my millionaire mentor:
- He grew up without a father.
- He grew up speaking Spanish.
- He is an immigrant from Cuba.
- He worked his way through a small state school for college.
- He came from the toughest, poorest, and most crime-ridden part of town.

Most would argue that, given his background, my mentor would have virtually NO chance at succeeding in life.

Yet, he proved every single person wrong.

- At 13, he had to start working to help his mother put food on the family table.
- At 24, he was fired from his first real job after working there for just two years.
- At 26, he started his first business, and went bankrupt after just four years.
- At 29, he started his second business, selling business health insurance.
- At 50, he sold his second business, netting $75 million in the process.
- At 51, he founded three new start-ups, specializing in health insurance.
- At 62, after growing his start-ups, he sold them at $50 million each.
- At 79, he continues his business ventures, running seven new start-ups.

Let's be real . . .

Based on how – and where – my mentor grew up, the odds of becoming somewhat successful, let alone a deca-millionaire and beyond were tiny.

Pretty much nonexistent.

But my mentor did not let a single doubter get in the way of starting his journey.

And what's even more crazy is that at almost age 80, he loves his work.

And work he does.

Every single day.

It's hard to tell that he is almost 80 years old because he continues to have a passion for what he does.

"My secret to getting rich?" He asked again, surprised by my direct question.

He sits back in the squeaky, wooden bakery chair and pushes his thin metal glasses up his nose, squinting at me as if he didn't know how to start answering my question.

After a long pause, he finally said, "It's not a secret, Fi," referring to my nickname (pronounced "fee"), which is short for my full name, Fiona.

"What do you mean?" I asked.

My mentor smiled and said, "I don't have a secret formula that will help you get rich. The only reason why I am where I am today is because of my purpose."

"Your purpose?" I was a little confused.

"I started my very first full-time job out of college at 24. I was a used car salesman. I hated every second of that job. I was paid decent money, but I hated my job."

My mentor took a sip of his hot tea.

"Why did you hate it so much?" I questioned.

"The truth, Fiona, is that I didn't have a purpose in that job.

All I did was sell used, overpriced cars to customers for a fat bonus check. That's it. There was no other reason for me to be in this job other than the money."

Slowly my mentor's words started making sense.

He continued, "Because I had no purpose in my job, I felt lost. I worked for the weekend. I dreaded Mondays. And I felt like I was in a prison. Those were the most boring, dullest years of my life."

Let me pause the story here.

Do you ever feel like:
- Your tie is your chain?
- Your cubicle is your prison cell?
- Your business suit is your prison jumpsuit?

If you said yes, then this book – and especially this chapter – is for you.

"So, what happened?" I asked.

"I got fired!" He chuckled, which was *not* the reaction I was expecting.

"My boss could tell how much I dreaded the job. So, he fired me. And honestly, I cannot thank my boss enough today. He did me a favor because if he didn't fire me back then, I don't think I would have been where I am today."

This part of our discussion had so much significance to me. Let me share why.

If you are worried about:

- Losing your job.
- Losing your friends.
- Losing your relationship.

. . . then remember this lesson:

Rejection is just another form of redirection in your life.

When you are rejected, try to understand why.

Learn from the rejection, and move on to bigger and better things.

"So what changed between the time you were fired and the time that you started your own business?" I had already finished my first cup of coffee at this point and had just ordered another one.

My mentor sat back into the old, wooden bakery chair and thought for a moment.

"I took some time off of work. I actually moved back with my mom. I had lost myself completely. Instead of focusing on my family, I focused on partying. Instead of caring for my mental health, I focused on the money. It was time I went back to my roots, and going back to where it all started was really where I found myself again."

And my mentor is right . . . sometimes you just have to go back to the basics if you feel like you're getting too far down the rabbit hole.

"At my mom's place, I finally had time to really take some time to think again for once. And that's where I found my purpose."

If I got a quarter for every time my mentor said the word *purpose*, I may have had a few dollars by now to pay for my coffees!

"Why do you place so much importance on finding your purpose?" I asked, almost done with my second cup of coffee.

"My purpose is the very reason why I do what I do. My purpose is the reason why I am so successful today."

I nodded, asking, "So what is your purpose?"

"Well, Fiona, it took me 26 years to figure that out. After my terrible experience working in corporate America, I went back home, to my roots, to have some time to think."

My mentor continued, "I knew that if I wanted to get anywhere in life, I needed to figure out the key that would unlock a burning desire and passion within me to succeed. And at 26, I was a very unmotivated fellow."

He laughed while he finished eating his croissant.

"One day, while I was caring for my aging mother at home, my purpose hit me like a baseball in the forehead," his eyes were distant, as if he was looking into his past so many decades ago.

"She had a bad fall. Hit her head on the wooden kitchen table and went unconscious. I didn't know what to do other than call 911. I have never felt so helpless and so scared in my life."

Sighing, he continued, "We couldn't afford the hospital bills because we couldn't afford insurance. We had no money. That fall destroyed my mom financially."

My mentor shook his head, crossed his arms, and sat up in his chair.

"That was when I realized I could not let another family go through what we were about to go through – financially, physically, emotionally, and mentally. That was when I knew my purpose."

He looked straight into my eyes, saying "My purpose is to help protect families from suffering financial ruin caused by medical bills."

And it's true.

The healthcare system in the United States is so expensive.

I once had a friend of mine break her arm through a random fall (while walking to the bathroom!) and without having health insurance, my friend had to pay $20,000 in medical bills!

Healthcare is *very* expensive in the United States.

Now my mentor had built his first business at 26, specializing as a door-to-door private health insurance agent.

He didn't study finance in school, either, and he didn't know what health insurance was before his mom had that tragic fall.

All he knew was that he wanted to help prevent people from facing financial ruin from medical injuries like his mother had.

"I stayed up late every night, studying to become a licensed health insurance agent. Every morning, I woke up at 4 a.m. to continue studying. I didn't do it because of the money – like my car sales job. I did it because I knew firsthand that one trip to the hospital can cost you everything you've ever worked for if you don't have the right health insurance."

My mentor's mom was in debt by over $150,000 after she was discharged from the hospital. She was healthy, but she had lost her life savings – and then some.

"But your first business wasn't successful . . . ? So maybe your purpose wasn't that strong?" I was looking for some guidance.

I really wanted to get a clear answer as to why my mentor became *so* successful.

"You're right, I completely failed at my first business. It was a disaster. I went knocking on our neighbors' doors, and received one yes for every 200 nos. Apparently everyone thought I was a dishonest insurance salesman and they had enough of me."

"But," he continued, "my first business taught me so many things about life. I learned how to negotiate, how to make friends and allies, and how to keep a keen eye on my business income – or in my case, business losses."

Experience really can help you build more knowledge than any formal education can.

Even if that experience is negative.

After failing – and going bankrupt – with his first business, at 29, my mentor had started his second business, which he would later sell at a net profit of $75 million.

"So tell me about your second business," I asked as I began to eat a fresh, chocolate-rich croissant the baker had just brought out for us.

"Well, I took the lessons I learned from my first business failure to heart. I realized that people just weren't interested in the service I was selling. But I knew I had to help people. It was my purpose. My mission. So, I started a new business, with a different structure, but the same mission."

At 29, my mentor had founded his second business, which specialized in selling affordable health insurance to small businesses.

His business had tapped into a hyper market niche, which did two things:

- His business was one of the pioneers to sell health insurance to small businesses.
- His business model stayed true to his purpose: helping people find affordable health insurance.

"The first three years in business were absolutely dreadful. I was so young that no one took me seriously. None of the CEOs and executives whom I pitched my business idea to thought I was bright enough. They didn't believe in me. At one point, I was even thinking about dying my hair gray so they would think I was older," he chuckled.

"But I believed in my purpose. I knew I had to help people – and I wasn't going to give up that easily," he continued.

And that's where it clicked for me.

I realized that to find success – whatever success may mean to you – you really do have to find your purpose first.

If you're only in it to earn money, you're doing it for the wrong reason. And chances are, you'll start dreading your job, just like my mentor did back when he was a car salesman.

You have to be in it for a greater reason than just money.

Sure, your 9 to 5 may pay your bills. But your day doesn't just stop at your 9 to 5 job. You have 16 more hours to your day.

Use those 16 additional hours to build a side business, network with like-minded people, or find a mentor who can unlock your inner potential.

When you find your purpose, every other aspect in your life will fall into place.

But here's the thing:

Finding your purpose isn't that easy.

Don't expect to sit down for a few minutes, think very hard, and then have a "lightbulb" moment where you identify your purpose.

It might take days.

Or weeks.

It might even take months to finally pinpoint your purpose.

And that's OK.

To help you get started, I've created an 8-Step Guide to Finding Your Purpose

1. Reflect on what people appreciate about you

Think about the feedback you receive from others.

- What do others appreciate about you?
- How do you help make a positive impact on their lives?

2. Find your community

Look at the people around you.

- What are their goals?
- What do you have in common?
- What is their impact on the world?

If your community inspires you, think about their purpose and how you can contribute to the impact they leave on the world.

3. Talk to one new person each week

Instead of only hanging out with the same people every day, try to expand your network.

Try to meet one new person each week – that's 52 new people in your network by the end of the year!

You could meet new people online or in person.

It might feel awkward and weird to start a conversation with someone new – but keep an open mind:

- You can learn new things.
- You can gain new perspectives.
- You can find new opportunities.

4. Try one new thing each weekend

Don't settle.

Dare to push your limits.

To find your purpose, you have to start being comfortable being uncomfortable.

The more you push yourself to learn new things, the more you find out about yourself, your likes, and your dislikes.

5. What makes you shudder at night?

Figure out what truly bothers you in this world.

- Is it an injustice?
- Is it animal cruelty?
- Is it homelessness?
- Is it a civil rights issue?
- Is it immigration policies?
- Is it about senior citizens?
- Is it people suffering from debt?

Take some time to think about what truly bothers you.

Perhaps you can make a difference in this world by finding what bothers you and by putting a stop to it.

6. What makes your heart skip a beat?

Take some time to truly reflect on what brings you joy.

- What do you enjoy?
- What makes your heart pound?
- What's something you do that is fun?
- What's something that you think about constantly?

That "thing" you think of constantly, that gets you going, and brings a smile to your face could actually be your purpose.

Sometimes, you just have to dig deep within yourself to find what you are truly passionate about.

7. What job would your 10-year-old self choose for you today?

Sometimes, we forget our childhood passions. We tend to have society and our life experiences squeeze our childhood dreams out of existence and replace them with dull, grim realities.

What if you could go back to your childhood passion and build that into a business?

Could that be your purpose?

It may or may not, but it's certainly worth revisiting your childhood dreams and exploring whether these could be recycled for your newfound purpose.

8. If you were to die two years from now, what would you want to be remembered for?

The two certain things in life are taxes and death. Your time is finite on this planet.

If you knew you were going to die in two years, what would you want to be remembered for?

Think about the following things:

- What do you value most?
- What is most important to you?
- What will your lasting legacy be?

Ultimately, finding your purpose comes down to working toward a mission that is bigger than yourself.

When you truly find your purpose, you will find peace in realizing that you are spending your finite time on this planet doing something that will leave a lasting legacy – no matter how big or how small.

My mentor told me his advice regarding purpose back when I was just about to head into college. But I only heard him, I didn't listen and understand.

Once I graduated from college, I worked for money.

Just like my mentor.

I joined a financial firm and worked as a wealth manager for the ultra-high-net-worth clients (typically ranging from $5 million to $100 million in net worth) for several years, helping the rich get richer.

It was a glamorous lifestyle:

- Being invited to elegant dinners.
- Playing golf with local celebrities.
- Getting a fat, bonus paycheck at the end of the year.

But let me tell you right now, **money doesn't buy happiness if you don't have your purpose**. Sure, it paid my bills, but my job left a hollow feeling inside of me.

Here was my truth:

- I felt like I lost all motivation.
- I hated golf (and I was terrible at it).
- I was always being judged by my colleagues.
- I am an introvert, so attending dinners was painful.
- I had to spend my bonus checks to keep up with my lifestyle.

I was working for a paycheck. Not for my purpose.

And after about five years of hard work, I realized I had to change something about my life or I would lead a very miserable, unfulfilled life.

My goal wasn't to help the rich get richer.

I wanted to make an impact in people's lives that *really* needed my help.

I knew I had to figure out what I wanted out of my life.

What my legacy was going to be.

And I went back to that conversation I had with my mentor and back to my roots – my family.

So I booked a flight over the upcoming Thanksgiving weekend. Four days of family time. Going back to my foundation. Where it all started.

During those four days away from work, I felt like my soul was being cleansed.

I felt like I could be myself again, away from the glitz and the glamour.

The Thanksgiving Day weekend was dreary and rainy, but it was exactly what I needed.

My true passion was helping the everyday person find their path to financial freedom.

A world where financial worries don't keep them up at night. A world where they can work toward their goals. A world where they understand basic financial ideas.

And that's when I closed one chapter of my life and opened another. I started building my financial planning platform: The Millennial Money Woman.

To find your purpose, first you have to explore new things, meet new people, and think new thoughts. If the old you didn't find a purpose, then you need to stop doing what the old you did. Push your limits; explore new depths.

In short: you have to be comfortable being uncomfortable.

Only then, when you push through new boundaries, are you able to find your true purpose and passion.

And when you find your purpose and passion, you can start anything, build anything, and do anything – regardless of the ups and downs.

That's because your actions are defined by your purpose.

Your life is defined by your purpose and when you find your purpose, your life will find you.

Challenge #1: Find Your Purpose

For this challenge, take some time and make it sacred.

1. Think about your purpose – have you found it already? Are you still searching for it?
2. If you haven't found your purpose, work through the 8-Step Guide.
3. Reflect on your current position in life and whether you're happy or unhappy.

Your purpose might not come to you by the end of this chapter. It might not even come to you by the end of this book, but keep thinking and keep digging.

It took my mentor 26 years to figure out his life's purpose – and it all happened by chance.

Be patient and be thoughtful, and soon enough, it will click and you'll know your purpose.

Chapter 3
Think of Money as Time, Not Money

Throughout my seven years as a wealth advisor, I had the privilege of working with 453 millionaires. About 98% of these millionaires were self-made.

And during my conversations with these millionaires, I learned a great deal about their mindset – especially when it came to their money mindset.

Chances are your best friend, your next door neighbor, or even your high school teacher think about money in a different way than millionaires do.

In fact, how do you think about money?

At this point, you're probably scratching your head because I just asked you a pretty odd question, right?

That's because most people think about money in terms of numbers, right?

For example, if Average Joe wants to buy $100 sneakers, then Average Joe is probably thinking about how much money he will have left after spending the $100.

Or how much total debt the $100 sneaker purchase will add to his existing credit card balance.

But my point is that Average Joe only thinks about that $100 expense as a number.

Nothing else.

And that, my friend, is exactly why Average Joe is average. And not a millionaire.

Because the millionaires whom I've worked with in the past all think about money in a different way.

They think about money as time. *Not* as money or numbers.

Here's an example:

Let's say you also want to buy those $100 sneakers that Average Joe was looking at.

And let's also say that you currently make $10 an hour working in a pizza shop.

Now the millionaire mindset would think how much *time* those sneakers would cost you – not how much money those sneakers would cost you.

So instead of these sneakers costing you $100, these sneakers will cost you 10 hours of your life.

Are sneakers worth 10 hours of your life?

Some of you might say no.

Others might say yes.

But the point is, by asking yourself how much of your *time* a particular purchase is worth, you may reconsider buying.

It's all about reframing your mindset when it comes to buying stuff.

And most of the self-made millionaires whom I've worked with have mastered their own mindset *before* building their wealth.

And if you want to build wealth, then start by reframing your thoughts on *how* you see money.

Connect the dollar value of a purchase with something much more intimate to your life – like the time you have left on this planet.

Numbers are cold, emotionless, and don't mean much.

But your time has so much more value and meaning.

If you're having trouble reframing your mindset when it comes to viewing money in terms of time, then I have a little tip for you:

Watch the movie *In Time*.

The movie *In Time* was released in 2011 and features Hollywood stars, including Amanda Seyfried and Justin Timberlake.

For those of you who have never seen the movie, I'm going to give you a brief synopsis (and no, my summary won't be a movie spoiler).

In Time Overview

- Science-fiction movie filmed in a dystopian the future.
- Instead of using money, the economic system in the movie uses time as a currency.
- You earn time by working and you lose time by buying goods or services, for example:
  - Each character has a clock on their arm counting down the amount of time they have left to live.

The movie is action-packed and has some unexpected twists, so I won't spoil it for those of you who haven't had the chance to see it.

But my point isn't about the plot of the movie.

My point is about the economic system that the movie's dystopian future society is built on: the fact that the currency is not money, as it is today, but that the currency of the future is, in fact, in time.

Take some time to truly think about this concept.

Perhaps time is not just the currency of some fictitious society of the future.

Perhaps there is a greater meaning to this movie.

Perhaps, time is already the currency of the present and we simply fail to recognize that significance.

Yes, we pay for our bills using money.

But think about how we earn that money.

We earn that money by spending our time working either for someone else or for ourselves.

Your time is finite, so don't waste it by spending it on things that don't add value to your life.

Every single person in this world has 24 hours in a day.

And it's really up to you to maximize the use of those 24 hours.

Maybe that means building a business on your own and working grueling hours for the first three years before your business takes off.

Or maybe that means getting another degree from the university, so you can increase your earnings in the future.

Or maybe that means putting more effort into your current job to earn a promotion.

Either way, every single person – from Bill Gates to Elon Musk to the late Steve Jobs and to the 453 millionaires I coached – only has 24 hours a day.

You do too.

Make the best of the time you have.

When I entered the workforce at age 21, I first was hired as an intern at a finance company.

There, I was probably earning around $10 an hour, working 40 paid hours a week. So that meant I was making around $1,600 a month (before taxes were taken out).

My income was pretty meager before I was offered a full-time position.

The following is a breakdown of my expenses and how many hours of my life I spent working to buy the goods and services that I bought.

Product or Service Bought	Cost in Dollars	Cost in Time
Rent – Apartment	$1,000 per month	100 hours
Cell Phone Bill	$114 per month	11.4 hours
Wi-Fi Bill	$77 per month	7.7 hours
Groceries	$300 per month	30 hours

Any income (and time) that isn't included in this monthly summary is taken out of my monthly income for taxes, social security, health insurance, and so on.

As you can see, I lived a pretty lean lifestyle back when I was an intern because I couldn't afford much on $10 an hour.

And I lived in a pretty expensive city.

When I started taking a closer look at *how* I spent my time on the things I bought each month, I was shocked.

Take a closer look at how [disproportionately] my time was allocated . . .

- I spent 62.5% of my time on rent.
- I spent 0% of my time on saving and investing.

Yikes!

If my goal was to become financially independent – which it was even as an intern at a finance company – then I had to *seriously* reconsider where I was currently in my life and how I was going to change my trajectory.

That's when I thought about how I could reallocate my time and pour it into something that would give my future substantial value.

And that, my dear reader, was how I moved away from spending my time (and money) on things that would *not* give me a long-term value.

Take a guess which area of spending I decided to cut first.

If you said rent, then you're 100% correct.

After reviewing how much money I was spending on rent (over 50% of my monthly income, which was ridiculous), I knew I had to act. Fast.

So, within the span of two to three months, I did the following:

- Got a roommate.
- Went thrift shopping.
- Went to discount grocery stores.
- Increased my savings and investments.

By getting a roommate and lowering my expenses on grocery stores, I cut my $1,000 monthly apartment price tag in half, saving about 50 hours of my life.

Every single hour of my life that I saved by decreasing my expenses (which turned out to be around 60 hours total), I used to save and invest for my future.

This massive mindset shift highlighted that I was finally using my time to build value for my future self. I wasn't simply "spending" my time on things that would have no lasting value (like rent).

Instead, I was spending more of my time (and consequently, my money) on what mattered most: *attaining financial freedom*.

By focusing on how much of my *time* I was spending on stuff, I ended up saving and investing close to *$600 per month*.

Once I was offered a full-time position at the finance company, my salary increased as well, which helped, of course.

But, I continued living my frugal lifestyle even as my salary increased.

And any "time" (and consequently money) that I saved, I put immediately into an investment account. But more on that later.

These healthy savings habits literally changed my life.

The mindset shift I made helped propel me ahead of most early 20-year-olds. By the age of 23, I had saved and invested enough to put a 20% down payment on my first home.

I won't go too in-depth on how I was able to buy a home at 23 (hint: I had some luck because I found a great deal and I brought some good negotiating skills to the table, which helped me drop the price substantially). But I do want to point out how a simple change in your mindset on how you think about money can make a *massive* difference in your overall financial picture.

Here's how thinking of money in terms of time can help improve your financial picture:
- You start spending money more consciously.
- You stop spending your money on things that don't add value to your life.

I find that when you tell people to budget, their eyes just glaze over. They don't want to hear another lecture about "budgeting" because – let's be real – budgeting is pretty boring.

Many people don't like dealing with numbers and many people feel uncomfortable when it comes to talking about money.

But, when you start talking about your time and how you spend your time, I see many people's eyes light up. By connecting the powerful emotions of money with time, the concept of saving money can become much easier.

No one wants to waste their time. Time is precious and every single person – regardless if you're Warren Buffett or a high school dropout – has 24 hours each and every day.

If you find yourself struggling to stay on a strict budget, think about the amount of time it takes you to earn the money so you can afford a good or service.

When you see that buying a pair of sneakers will cost 100 hours of your time, you may want to reconsider your purchase.

Is 100 hours of your life really worth a pair of sneakers? Probably not.

Going back to the movie *In Time,* the characters could "spend" their time on goods and services. Every instance they spent a portion of their remaining time on something, you could see their life clock lose minutes of their life.

The movie, like most movies, is exaggerated and obviously science fiction, but the moral of the story still holds true:

Be careful how you use your money. You will never get back the time you spend to earn that money.

Now that you know why it's a good idea to connect the ideas of money with your time, let's take a closer look into how you can become a master budgeter.

Challenge #2: Think of Money as Time, Not Money

For this challenge, put away your phone, your computer, and so on, and dedicate this time to moving one step closer to your financial goals.

1. Think about how much you earn monthly.
2. Think about how much you spend monthly.
3. Think about how much time your expenses cost you.

When you connect the amount of time it takes you to make the money to buy something, you'll never think of money the same again.

Now try cutting some of your monthly recurring expenses that don't make your life better.

After I changed my mindset to think of money as time and not just money, I saw the price of my expenses as the price of my life.

And that helped me change my spending lifestyle for good.

Chapter 4
Stealth Wealth

How many times have you seen a celebrity or a model flash their bling in front of the camera?

Maybe your favorite Instagram influencer just posted 100 pictures of herself in front of her Bugatti or Ferrari or Porsche.

Or maybe they were taking a selfie in front of a private jet plane with their Louis Vuitton purse and Dolce & Gabbana oversized sunglasses while holding their crème-colored pet Chihuahua in their Prada purse.

OK, enough name drops.

But you get the point, right?

Online influencers and celebrities in general like flashy stuff.

They like to show off their things.

And often times, the modern person believes that if you show off expensive name brands like YSL, Ferragamo, Chanel, Gucci, Fendi, Armani . . . just to name a few . . . that means YOU ARE RICH.

That you've made it.

And the sad thing?

The idea that you're rich just because you're wearing or buying luxury things COULD NOT be further from the truth.

Showing off "nice" things doesn't necessarily mean you are richer than your next-door neighbor.

In fact, it could mean you are worse off. Poorer, in fact.

How?

Think about it:

If you have all of these nice, luxury things like a Gucci purse, for example, that means your money is no longer in your investment or savings account.

Your money was spent on a material item that very likely will be depreciating and losing value over time because you are *using* that item.

So because you bought this Gucci purse for $5,000, you are arguably $5,000 poorer than before.

Of course, if you are a luxury item investor and plan to resell the purse for more money in the future – then that's another story.

But I'm not talking investing in luxury goods.

I'm talking about spending money on luxury things to look rich to impress people who don't care.

Just like Dave Ramsey's popular quote goes:

"We buy things we don't need with money we don't have to impress people we don't like."

For me, that saying hits hard.

Now, what's one common theme that you think of when you hear the names of these celebrities?

- 50 Cent
- Mike Tyson
- Nicolas Cage
- MC Hammer
- Michael Jackson
- Floyd Mayweather

Most people would associate each of these celebrities with money.

But you know what?

Each and every one of these celebrities went bankrupt.

Yep.

And yet, because you see them wearing flashy clothes, driving nice cars, and living in luxury mansions, you would think they are rich.

But think again.

The popular 1990s rapper 50 Cent allegedly owed more than $32.5 million.

The heavyweight champion Mike Tyson apparently owed more than $40 million in debt (even though he earned about $400 million over his career).

The award-winning actor Nicolas Cage built a $150 million fortune and ended up owing money to the IRS.

The legendary singer MC Hammer reportedly went $13 million into debt after making frivolous purchases like buying a $1-million mansion but making about $30 million worth of adjustments to the place, staffing the home with 200 people, and buying a 19-racehorse stable. Talk about wasting money!

The King of Pop, Michael Jackson, was said to owe between $400 and $500 million before his death.

And one of the most successful fighters of all time, Floyd Mayweather allegedly owed a reported $22.2 million to the IRS.[1]

Are you shocked?

I sure was when I first saw how much debt these supposed "rich" celebrities were in.

So what's the moral of this story here?

If you see other people showing off flashy, expensive items, that doesn't necessarily mean they are rich.

In fact, I've found that most of the time, the people who do show off flashy Louis Vuitton purses, sunglasses, or even suitcases are the ones who have high credit card debt.

I know it might sound counterintuitive, but that's typically the case.

I mean, think about it.

How often do you see truly wealthy icons like:

- Elon Musk,
- Carlos Slim,
- Warren Buffett, and . . .

Flash their wealth?

So what do these three people have in common?

First, they are all billionaires and the wealthiest people in the world.

Second, they don't flash their wealth.

For example, Elon Musk, who once again was the wealthiest person in the world as of mid-2023, sold every single house he owned in his $100-million real estate empire and now lives in a very small, $50,000 home that he rents from his company SpaceX.

Warren Buffett, who is the sixth wealthiest person in the world, still lives in the same house he bought back in 1958 for a whopping $31,500. He could have bought $100-million mansions if he wanted to, but he still owns his original house.

Carlos Slim is the wealthiest man in Mexico – by a long shot – and he doesn't indulge in yachts, jets, or flashy Ferraris. Instead, he drives an old Mercedes-Benz and has lived in the same house for more than 40 years.

Each of these billionaires has more money than you and I can probably ever dream of.

And yet, they live more frugally than probably some of us.

As you can see, if you have a lot of money, you don't need to show it off.

In fact, most people who have a lot of money – regardless if they are at the billionaire or millionaire level – don't actually have the need to show off their wealth.

They follow the motto Stealth Wealth.

Instead of spending their money on flashy things to impress people, they walk like the Average Joe. They buy regular clothes. They live in average neighborhoods. They drive normal cars.

The only thing that's not normal is the value of their bank account.

And there's a good reason why: instead of spending their money, they keep it saved and invested.

I like to think of stealth wealth like the popular saying goes:

Wealth is quiet.
Rich is loud.
Poor is flashy.

If your goal is to become wealthy over the long term, then start living by this motto.

Challenge #3: Stealth Wealth

Hopefully this chapter shares a little more insight into the mindset of a true self-made millionaire:

They typically don't have the need to show off their money.
True millionaires follow the Stealth Wealth rule.
They act like normal people.
They spend money on normal things.
But what's abnormal is their bank and investment account.

So here's your next challenge

If you want to build true wealth, then try to be a little more conscious with your spending.

For example, if you find yourself buying a Prada purse just because your best friend showed off hers on Instagram, then try to yell the word "STOP!" in your mind.

Picture a big, red stop sign, if you will.

Visualize yourself coming to a firm halt.

Now I want you to remember the saying I mentioned earlier:

Wealth is quiet.
Rich is loud.
Poor is flashy.

(Continued)

And ask yourself if you *really* need that Prada handbag.
Is it really worth $1,000 (or whatever they typically cost)?
Or can you keep living the stealth wealth life of an undercover millionaire?

While you're still visualizing that big, flashing stop sign in your mind, start thinking about WHAT is more important to you:

- Buying an expensive and depreciating item?
- Saving and investing the money for your future?

Here's how much that $1,000 Prada handbag would cost you over the next 25 years

If you had invested that $1,000 in the stock market instead at an average annual rate of return of about 7% (which is pretty conservative), over 25 years, that $1,000 would have turned to: $5,427.43.

Now go out there and live the life of an undercover millionaire!

Note

1. Acevedo, M.M., Angélica. (2019). 25 celebrities who were rich and famous before losing all their money. [online] *Business Insider.* https://www.businessinsider.com/rich-famous-celebrities-who-lost-all-their-money-2018-5#floyd-mayweather-jrs-nickname-is-money-for-never-losing-a-boxing-match-ironically-he-owed-money-to-the-irs-3 (accessed 1 July 2023).

Chapter 5
Pay Yourself First

When I was young (and even now), I loved taking road trips across the country. Road trips were my absolute favorite (mainly because I didn't have to drive the car!). I would look out of the car window, see the scenery rushing past, and all the colors blurred into one.

The road trips we took as a family are actually a very sweet part of my childhood.

And the best part about the many road trips we took?

I absolutely LOVED eating the many unique flavors of food . . . from the traditional New England clam chowder to the delicious Texas Barbecue to homey Southern grits to Chicago Deep-Dish Pizzas.

Have you ever taken a road trip?

Even if you've never taken a road trip before, I want you to think about *how* you managed to drive from one place to the other.

Chances are, you had to use a map.

Or a navigation system.

Or your iPhone.

Or a compass.

The point is, most of us don't have an internal GPS, where we could navigate around the world without needing a map.

And if you know me, you'd realize how bad I am at navigating (even if I have TWO navigation systems working at the same time).

Now, my family and I wouldn't have made a single successful road trip from Point A (home) to Point B (our destination), without:

- A road map.
- Reviewing the navigation system.
- Preparing meals and snacks for the trip.

We planned ahead so that once our road trip started, everything would run smoothly.

And luckily, it always did!

So why are we talking so much about road tripping?

That's because the whole road trip process – from preparing for a road trip to hopping into your car to navigating the car to arriving safely at your destination – is *just* like building wealth.

In fact, I would argue that if you don't prepare properly for a long road trip (like with a navigation system, snacks, and packing all of your bags), you probably will encounter some obstacles.

And that's *exactly* what you have to do, if you want to build wealth.

Specifically, before your paycheck hits your bank account you *have* to plan and prepare for your money.

If there's one major lesson I learned by working with 453+ millionaires, it was that rich people plan.

They plan all the time.

They plan their week in advance.

They plan their vacations in advance.

They plan their next 20 years in advance.

They plan how to run their business in advance.

And more importantly, they also plan how to use their money in advance.

And that's why rich people are rich.

OK, so what does all of this have to do with this chapter's title "Pay Yourself First"?

The first time I heard this phrase, I thought paying yourself first meant buying fancy clothing, eating out, and spending lavishly BEFORE spending any money on bills.

LOL.

Boy, was I wrong!

So don't worry if you don't know what "pay yourself first" means either. That's why I'm writing this chapter for you.

So what does it mean?

When you pay yourself first, you save/invest your paycheck money *before* you spend it on bills.

In other words, you're already planning what happens to your money before you actually get it.

And believe me, having a plan in place (like for your road trips) is pretty important to success. The same goes for building wealth: having a plan in place for how you intend to spend your money will make the greatest difference.

So why is paying yourself first a wealth-building mindset?

It really comes down to our human nature. . . .

Think about it:

Why do we not wake up at 3 in the morning and go running for 30 miles straight before going to work?

Because we're lazy.

I know that most of us could do that if we trained enough and put our minds to it.

In fact, if you know of David Goggins, then you know that it is 100% possible to wake up at a ridiculously early time and run.

So why don't I do it?

And why don't you do it?

I'm going to say the cold, hard truth: You and I are both lazy.

It's not an insult, but it's the reality.

In fact, humans in general are lazy, right?

For example, we all know that exercising is so important to our mental, emotional, and physical well-being.

Yet most of us don't exercise.

It takes A LOT of will power to get out of our comfortable lives, put on those gym clothes, and start working out. I admit it – I struggle with it myself.

In fact, I go so far as to wear a shirt that literally says, "I Hate Running" every time I go running on the treadmill or outside in nature because I actually hate running.

Anyone who sees me run with that shirt cracks a smile and I think it's pretty funny myself.

But let's get back to the point.

We humans will do what's *easiest* for us, and not what's *best* for us. In other words, it's easier to spend money than it is to save money.

And the rich understand this secret.

They understand that humans are naturally attracted to the easy route.

And that's why the rich try to outsmart themselves by *automating* their lives to build long-term wealth.

The rich do not rely on "just" willpower to save and invest.

In fact, relying on willpower is *not* a good strategy. Willpower fades, but discipline lasts.

Knowing that willpower fades, the rich automate their savings and investments.

By automating their saving and investment strategies, the rich don't have to take another second to think about building long-term wealth.

Instead, they can use their brain power, time, and energy to do whatever it is that they do best – make money.

Automating your lifestyle is the easy way – but it's also the smart way to building wealth.

And you don't have to be raking in $200,000 per year to do that or already be a millionaire.

Even if you have a negative net worth, you can start automating your financial lifestyle – like by automatically making contributions from your paycheck to your 401k.

Here's what you'll have to do:
- Calculate how much money you want saved/invested.
- Calculate where your money should be invested/saved (e.g., Roth IRA, 401k, emergency savings account, etc.).
- Calculate how often you want to invest your money (weekly, semi-weekly, monthly, etc.).

And trust me, you want to figure out these three steps as early as possible.

That's because time is your best friend and greatest ally.

The earlier you save and invest, the faster you will build your wealth, which means you can retire earlier and enjoy your life more!

Since I started learning the way of the millionaire, I began living my life by the phrase "pay yourself first."

Instead of getting my paycheck first and *then* determining how to allocate my money, I predetermine *exactly* how my money should be distributed (whether to investment accounts or to my checking account, for instance).

The following are some accounts that I automatically invest in, every week:

- My Roth IRA.
- My Roth Solo 401k.
- My HSA (health savings account).
- My Emergency Savings fund (although this is currently fully funded).

The less I have to think about *how* to manage my money, the better.

And trust me, this is how 94% of the self-made millionaires whom I've worked with operate as well.

They are lazy.

Because it's human nature.

But they engineer their laziness to help them make money.

By automating their finances.

And so, they become lazy millionaires.

I'll be honest with you, if it wasn't for automating my investments and my savings, I probably wouldn't be in the financial position that I am in today.

Do yourself a favor and automate your wealth.

Even if that means you're auto-investing "just" $5 every month.

That's OK.

Because you're starting to form a rich habit.

And as you make more money, you can increase your automatic savings.

Here are some of the steps I took (and you can too) to automate wealth:
- First, I researched and chose an investment platform.
- Second, I opened my investment accounts.
- Third, I connected my savings account with my investment accounts.
- Next, I selected the frequency, amount, and the type of investment (if applicable) I wanted to buy.
- Finally, I hit "submit order request" and the rest is history, as they say!

While setting up an automatic investment strategy might be a little bit of work, that's probably the *most* amount of time you'll have to put in.

The rest, is automated.

I've seen many first-time investors enjoy the automatic investing features that many investment platforms offer – regardless if they are the "traditional" brokers (like Fidelity, Charles Schwab, Vanguard, etc.) or if they are the "newer" robo-advisor platforms (like M1 Finance or Acorns, e.g.).

If you're unable to find the automatic investing function, then consider calling customer service or emailing your account representative.

And the best part?

To start "paying yourself," you don't actually need ANY money to open an account.

In fact, there are several robo-advisor and "traditional" platforms that let you open an investment account with $0.

I'm saying this because there is NO MORE EXCUSE.

So what if you don't have any money right now to invest?

So what if you don't have $100 to invest?

That's OK!

Just open an account first.

Have it be the "shell account" so it's ready when you do have $5 or $20 to invest.

In the words of the famous Nike slogan: "Just Do It."

And if you're still doubting that a small contribution can make a big difference in the future, then check out this future value calculation of how you can build wealth by investing just $1 every single day for 40 years:

Amount invested	$1
Investment period	Daily
Investment return	7%
Length of time	40 years
Ending portfolio value	$80,509.79
Actual dollar contributions	$14,600

As you can see, if you were to invest (not save) just $1 per day for 40 years, you would have about $80,000 . . . .

And that's ALL thanks to the magic of compounding interest (which we'll discuss later).

What's even better is that of the $80,000, only $14,600 is actually YOUR money (from your $1 a day contributions).

The other $65,909.79 is 100% from compounding investment growth.

As you can see from this very simple example, when you are investing, the most important factor to your success is *time*.

And the earlier you start investing, the better it is for you.

That's one of the key secrets to building wealth – and paying yourself first by automating everything will get you there faster.

If you continue paying yourself first, then by the time you retire, you'll have a high chance of having enough money to supplement your lifestyle needs.

Typically, it's recommended you have about 10 to 20 times of your annual income saved.

Sadly, however, not everyone realizes how important it is to start saving and investing for retirement from an early age.

In fact, 21% of Americans aren't saving *anything* for retirement.[1]

And even worse, for those who do save and invest for retirement, they just aren't doing enough.

In fact, the other day, I was speaking to someone who was hoping to retire in 10 years but was only investing $25 per paycheck and had about $5,000 saved. That's unfortunately not enough to live the life you want.

To keep up with inflation, it is estimated that you'll have to save a minimum of 10% to 17% of your annual income – and that's assuming you start saving at age 25.

Now, I personally disagree with that estimate.

My rule of thumb is to save *at least* 20% of your annual income.

In fact, I started saving and investing around 70% of my gross annual income. While I know that number is not possible for everyone and is a bit on the extreme side, I do want to show you just *how important* it is to save more when you're young to get ahead.

I know it might be difficult to give up on some of life's pleasures (like going to bars, eating out, going on long vacations, etc.) in your twenties just to save and invest.

It was for me too.

In fact, I often felt left out from my group of friends because they enjoyed eating out and partying and buying new things.

But then I realized something.

I realized that I was hanging out with the WRONG group of friends!

So I started looking for my own crowd.

The crowd that would have a similar mindset. That would work as hard as me to achieve financial freedom.

Because remember that if you want to be above average, you will have to do what the average person will not.

And as you know, the data clearly shows that the average person does not save more than 20% of annual income.

Even if you are unable to save 20% of your total annual income because you have debt, kids, or other bills – that's still not an excuse to not save *anything*.

Every dollar matters.

And as you saw in the $1 a day investing example, every dollar really does make a difference.

Let's circle back to my story about the road trips I used to take as a child.

I wanted to share another valuable lesson I learned from my family road trips.

And if you have trouble sleeping at night because you're worried about money or if you are worried about coming up with the money for a potential future unexpected bill, then you may want to keep reading.

The rich, as I have learned, are masters in paying themselves first by also managing their risk exposure.

What does this mean?

The rich plan and prepare for risks.

If they have an unexpected expense like:

- A flat tire,
- A roof replacement, or
- Medical emergencies

. . . then the last thing the rich do is put those expenses on their credit cards. However, another strategy is using their credit cards to pay for emergencies, gain credit card points, and then pay off the credit card debt before the bill is due.

Typically, though, the rich use their emergency savings funds to help them prepare and manage unexpected expenses.

Rich people stay out of debt by building up an emergency savings fund.

And an emergency savings fund is a liquid and easily accessible savings account. You'll want to save 3 to 6 months' worth of your living expenses in cash to be used only for emergencies.

Sadly, though, not many actually build an emergency savings fund.

In fact, 63% of Americans cannot come up with the cash to cover a $500 emergency.[2] Yikes!

Don't fall into this statistic.

The good news is that you can avoid becoming this statistic by paying yourself first – specifically by building up your emergency savings account.

Typically, the wealthy pay themselves first by stashing cash in an emergency savings fund. Once their emergency savings account is fully funded, the rich continue paying themselves first – just moving money into their investment accounts instead.

If you find you don't have enough in your emergency savings account (the rule of thumb is 3 to 6 months' worth of living expenses), then I would suggest focusing the majority of your efforts on boosting your emergency savings account first (assuming you've already paid off debt).

Then worry about investing.

To earn the most on your emergency savings fund cash, you may want to consider opening a high-yield savings account, where the interest you earn on your cash is typically higher than the interest rate you would earn on any regular savings account.

And the rich keep paying themselves first by using a high-yield savings account for their emergency savings account.

The interest rates on high-yield savings accounts are typically much higher than regular savings accounts.

In fact, in a few cases, I've seen that high-yield savings accounts have interest rates increased by about 198% than in regular savings accounts!

Talk about getting the biggest bang for your buck through passive income.

Here are the typical characteristics of high-yield savings accounts (but make sure you check out the fine print before you sign up yourself):

- Online
- Low to no fees
- FDIC insurance
- Higher interest rates
- Low to no minimum deposits

Just keep in mind that the interest rates for high-yield savings accounts do actually change over time with the economic landscape – because they are variable.

So, for example, during a very low interest rate environment (such as during the 2020 and 2021 years), high-yield savings accounts also didn't have high-interest rates (typically around 0.7%).

However, during higher interest rate environments (such as during 2022 and 2023), high-yield savings accounts increased their interest rates (typically between 4% and 5%).

Challenge #4: Plan for Your Paycheck and Prepare for Emergencies

For this challenge, think back to a family road trip that you took.

Try to think about the planning that went into the road trip (even if it was minimal – like taking a water bottle or a snack for the trip).

Now take some time to think about how you can best plan and prepare for your paycheck.

Just like a road trip, you'll probably be MUCH more successful in building wealth if you have an existing plan in place for how you will use every dollar of your paycheck before the money even hits your bank account.

Now, I want you to ask yourself the following questions:

- Are you paying yourself first?
- If so, how much?
- Do you have an emergency savings account that could cover 3 to 6 months' worth of your living expenses?

And worse, what if you lost your job – would you feel comfortable that the cash in your emergency savings fund would hold you over until you found a new job?

(Continued)

Be honest with yourself and plan accordingly.

1. Think about whether you are planning for each paycheck and paying yourself first.
2. Consider how much you are saving and investing currently – is it enough to match the minimum of saving 10% to 17% of your annual income?
3. Determine whether you have 3 to 6 months' worth of living expenses saved in your emergency savings fund.

Remember this: To become a millionaire, you must plan for your paycheck.

Willpower and motivation will last you only for a limited time.

That's why you should consider automating your investment and savings strategy today.

Notes

1. Napoletano, E. (2023) How much should you save for retirement? *Forbes*. Available at: https://www.forbes.com/advisor/retirement/how-much-to-save-for-retirement/#:~:text=It's%20no%20secret%20that%20most, aren't%20saving%20at%20all. (Accessed: 02 September 2023).
2. McGrath, M. (2016). 63% of Americans don't have enough savings to cover a $500 emergency. [online]. *Forbes*. https://www.forbes.com/sites/maggiemcgrath/2016/01/06/63-of-americans-dont-have-enough-savings-to-cover-a-500-emergency/?sh=3b370e874e0d (accessed 1 July 2023).

Chapter 6
Growth versus Fixed Mindset

How many of you like running?

As you may remember from a previous chapter, I'm not a big fan of running . . . in fact, when I run, I actually wear a shirt that says "I Hate Running" when I go on runs!

LOL.

But I did have quite a few friends who were top-tier runners in high school.

In fact, one of my friends got into an Ivy League school on a cross-country running scholarship because she was a top runner in her state.

So what was her secret?

I decided to reach out and sit down with her for a coffee chat.

My friend Alexa was an average teenager who never really put too much effort into competing in cross country or other running competitions.

In fact, she always considered herself to be one of the slowest in her group, until the high school hired a new track and cross-country running coach. Let's call her Coach Kya.

It was Coach Kya who completely transformed my friend from an average runner into one of the top three in the state and got my friend a full scholarship ride into an Ivy League school.

How did Coach Kya change my friend from average to above average?

Well, that's exactly the question I asked my friend during our coffee chat one rainy afternoon.

We were sitting in a cozy coffee shop that smelled of freshly ground coffee beans. We were lounging on a wooden bench, in the corner, that gently creaked every time you moved. The sky outside was a dark gray color with rain streaming down the thick glass window panes. A rhythmic, rolling thunder was heard every few minutes or so. There was no one else in the coffee shop, aside from the barista who was leaning against the coffee counter, scrolling through her phone, and jamming out to mid-20th-century jazz music.

"So, what's the secret?" I asked my friend Alexa.

She smiled while taking a long sip from her caramel latte.

"It has to do with your brain," she said pointing to her forehead. "Whether you win in a sport, or really in anything, comes down to your mindset."

That was a lightbulb moment for me.

You really can do anything if you have the right mindset.

Alexa continued saying, "Coach Kya told me that 80% of winning in cross-country has to do with mindset. And the other 20% has to do with talent."

Alexa paused.

"And you know what else I found out, Fiona?"

I shook my head.

"The biggest battle in any competition is within. It's with yourself," Alexa looked me dead in the eye.

"You're not competing against the other racers. If you really want to be the best out there, the fight is actually with yourself. You have to outperform yourself. You have to *really* want it. Only then, will you win."

Alexa pushed her glasses up her nose and continued, "Coach Kya made me memorize the words of Henry Ford: "Whether you think you can or think you can't, you're right." And that saying made a world of a difference to me."

Henry Ford's saying gave me goosebumps.

"Whether you think you can or think you can't, you're right."

Wow.

I want you to put down this book and close your eyes.

Think about what this simple saying from Henry Ford actually means. What it stands for.

To me, it symbolizes grit. Perseverance. Willpower. And most importantly, mindset.

It doesn't matter if you're a cross-country runner like my friend Alexa or if you're a mathematician or if you're someone who is looking to save their next $100.

Whether you are successful – or not – really does depend on your mindset.

And that's exactly what this chapter is about.

Your mindset.

****

Dr. Carol S. Dweck is arguably one of the most popular psychology researchers of our time.

She has won multiple awards for her contributions to developmental psychology, social psychology, and personality psychology.

The first time I read Dr. Dweck's book *Mindset: The New Psychology of Success* was in my entrepreneurship class in college.

The thin, 320-page paperback book contains *so* much wisdom.

Dr. Dweck's book discusses the two prominent types of mindsets, one of which is the mindset that Alexa referred to earlier, during our coffee chat:

- Fixed mindset, and
- Growth mindset.

Can you guess which mindset Coach Kya taught Alexa?

Dr. Dweck explores each mindset – the fixed mindset and the growth mindset – separately and then discusses why one mindset prevents success and why the other promotes success.

The fixed mindset, as I am sure you have guessed by now, halts growth. It actually keeps you stagnant and prevents you from optimizing your full potential.

If you have a fixed mindset, then you believe that you cannot improve the qualities you were given from birth. You believe your knowledge or ability fixed. You also believe that success is a result of natural talent and not hard work.

People with a fixed mindset typically never reach their full potential.

They stop growing and plateau early in their careers because they believe that becoming successful is based on natural talent and not so much on dedication and hard work.

Dr. Dweck emphasizes that growth *cannot* be achieved without stepping outside of your comfort zone.

And to grow, you must be comfortable being uncomfortable.

Only when you step outside of your comfort zone will you experience rapid progress, which is the very definition of the growth mindset, which is the second type of mindset explored in Dr. Dweck's book.

If you have a growth mindset, then you believe that you can improve the qualities you were given from birth. You believe you can grow your knowledge or talent through pushing yourself outside of your comfort zone and experience.

Typically speaking, if you identify as someone with a growth mindset, then you're someone who is putting in hard work to become successful.

To become successful with a growth mindset – however you define *success* – you know that you will become better through experience, time, and learning from failure.

To help you better understand the two types of mindsets, I illustrate some key qualities, below:

Fixed Mindset:
- Quits early.
- Fears failure.
- Avoids feedback.
- Wants to look smart.
- Thinks personal knowledge is fixed.
- Believes effort is worthless.
- Is threatened by accomplishments of others.

On the other hand, the following is a snapshot of growth mindset characteristics:

Growth Mindset:
- Embraces failure.
- Embraces feedback.
- Wants to learn more.
- Perseveres during setbacks.
- Believes hard work is part of success.
- Is inspired by accomplishments of others.

Take some time to read through both lists and think about which mindset you identify with most.

If you feel that you already embody the traits of the growth mindset, then you are ahead of the curve.

If you believe you identify with some of the fixed mindset qualities, then you are not alone.

In fact, back in college when I first read *Mindset: The New Psychology of Success*, I actually identified with more than 50% of the fixed mindset traits.

Yikes.

And to be honest with you, I was pretty embarrassed to learn that I identified more with the fixed mindset than with the growth mindset – since I knew it was better to have a growth mindset. So if you feel like you're in the same boat as I was back then, that's totally OK.

It's actually pretty normal to identify as someone with a fixed mindset.

I mainly identified as a fixed mindset personality because of my constant need to prove myself (and ultimately, be accepted by others).

And I saw every single result of mine as either a success or a failure – and I was terrified of failing. There was no "gray" area for me. It was black and white. Win or lose.

And a for a typical fixed mindset individual, there are only two outcomes:

- Success, or
- Failure.

For a growth mindset, you don't associate a failure as a negative. Instead, you begin to embrace failure as a learning opportunity so you can improve for the next time.

Now I'm sure you're asking yourself the same question I did back when I read Dr. Carol Dweck's book for the first time: Can you change from a fixed mindset to a growth mindset?

And the answer is: Absolutely.

The very first step is actually recognizing which mindset you currently embody, which we just did.

The next step is figuring out a roadmap to change your mindset. **And to change your reality, start by changing your mentality.**

So if you hear your inner mind saying things like:

- I can't do this.
- I'm going to fail.
- This will take forever.

You first have to physically tell yourself "Stop!"
Here's what I did to overcome this negative inner dialogue:

- First, I closed my eyes.
- Then, I pictured a big, red stop sign.
- Finally, I forced myself to shift my negative thoughts to something neutral (like walking my dog in nature).

This mental exercise may sound a bit odd, but it actually works for me.

Basically, you are trying to steer your conscious mindset away from a negative inner dialogue. And remember that what you feed your *subconscious* mind is often how you start to think about yourself and about life *consciously*.

The very *last* thing you want to do is tell yourself something negative (like "I can't do this") and then actually start to believe it!

That's why it is *imperative* to stop yourself from thinking these negative thoughts.

Now, you can do whatever exercise or routine best works for your situation – whether that's imagining a big red stop sign or whether that's going for a short walk whenever you think a negative thought.

Whatever works for you.

But the key to changing from a fixed mindset to a growth mindset has to do with consistency.

It has to do with building an actual habit.

And as many of you know, building a habit to the point where it becomes second nature and you don't consciously have to think about it, can take anywhere from three weeks to three months – or longer.

That's why it's SO important to start following your system – whatever it may be – *consistently*.

Next, implement some of these steps to switch your fixed mindset thinking to a growth mindset thinking:
- Embrace failure.
- Learn from feedback.
- Accept your imperfections.
- Discover different strategies.
- Consider challenges as opportunities.

Although there are many, many additional steps you can take to readjust your thinking from a fixed mindset to a growth mindset, these steps are a good place to start.

But to change your mentality, it will take time.

Don't expect to see immediate results overnight.

Just like my friend Alexa said during our coffee chat that rainy and thunderous afternoon, whether you think you can or you can't, you're right.

It just depends on how *badly* you want it.

Like I said before, I am so thankful I read Dr. Dweck's book, because it really did help me change my reality from an early age.

If you want to obtain a winning mindset, whether that has to do with money, building a business, or simply with life in general, then a great place to start is by adopting a *growth mindset*.

Challenge #5: Adopt a Growth Mindset

For this challenge, take some time to think about the two mindsets mentioned in this chapter: The **growth mindset** and the **fixed mindset**.

Determine whether you embody the characteristics of the growth mindset or the fixed mindset (it could be that you have characteristics of both).

Be honest with yourself.

Is there one mindset that you identify with more than the other?

If you feel like you identify with more of the fixed mindset characteristics (just like I did), then take some time to read through some of the steps I listed to help you start changing from a fixed mindset to a growth mindset:

1. Determine if you embody characteristics of a fixed mindset or a growth mindset
2. Read through my list of action steps to help you change your thinking from a fixed to a growth mindset
3. Read the book *Mindset: The New Psychology of Success* for better insight and more context

Remember this

To become successful in life – whether that means becoming a millionaire or becoming a top-notch business owner – you *must* adopt a growth mindset.

With a growth mindset, you can win at almost anything.

Your knowledge, intelligence, and talent is never fixed. With enough effort, time, and experience, you will improve. It just takes patience and the belief that you can *always* change to thrive. Nothing in this world is static – unless you believe it.

Chapter 7
Find a High-Quality Mentor

Have you ever heard of the saying "a mentor is the ultimate shortcut to life?"

Maybe you haven't.

But the saying is 100% true.

I have been very fortunate to have had several incredible mentors over the course of my life.

And the truth is, you'll never know exactly *where* you'll meet your future mentor.

It could be at a mall, at a dog park, or as in my case, volunteering at a local nonprofit organization.

I always had a passion for education and helping people better understand money matters because I knew from personal experience how *difficult* life can be if you don't have a knowledge of finance.

So, I started volunteering in local organizations, teaching young kids and adults the basics of money management. I enjoyed what I was doing so much that I decided to join the board of this non-profit organization.

Taking a seat at the board table was like taking a seat with some of the coolest, most generous people in the world.

The people who generally participate on board seats are experienced business leaders, owners, or managers, and have some valuable life skills they can bring to the nonprofit community.

This particular board had 13 seats total, and I was the youngest person probably by about 30 years or so!

That didn't intimidate me, however.

I took that as a sign to jump in head-first and get to know each and every board member by inviting them to a quick lunch over the course of the year.

Why did I decide to spend money for lunch with every board member?

First of all, I read through every board member's biography (which is typically published on the nonprofit's website). And I identified which board members in particular I wanted to get to know better.

And second of all, who doesn't like getting a free lunch?!

It's a great way to connect with people, eat good food, and still work toward a shared mission and goal: helping your nonprofit.

During one of my lunches, I pretty much made an immediate connection with an elderly business owner who had served on the board for the last 20 years.

He was very passionate in the board's mission to educate young children about finance because this board member himself also had a difficult childhood growing up due to lack of financial literacy knowledge.

He was successful, had made a lot of money during his career as a businessman, and was ready to give back to the community.

He would become the most influential mentor of my life.

And our connection grew during our first lunch.

I invited him to a local lunch hot spot, and simply wanted to get to know *him*. I didn't have any agenda in mind – like asking him to officially become my mentor (while that idea did cross my mind at one point, I did not bring up the mentor question during our first lunch).

My very first goal was simply to get to know *him*.

I wanted to find out this person's story, his ambitions, his passions, his successes, and of course, what future he envisioned for the nonprofit. In fact, our conversation started off by discussing our common interest: helping the nonprofit.

From there, our conversation swerved into different directions, from discussing animal welfare to discussing career and business advice. It was at that point when I realized our goals lined up, our personalities lined up, and of course, our passions also resembled each other.

Now, listen up, especially if you're looking to find a high-quality mentor.

First, don't ask them to do something for you immediately (like being your mentor) during the lunch. That makes you seem two-faced.

Second, soon after you have had lunch with your potential mentor, take 10 minutes and actually write them a hand-written thank-you note.

Genuinely thank them for taking the time to eat lunch with you.

Chances are, the people whom you invite to lunch are probably very successful. So let's face the truth: Every minute and every hour that they spend away from their work is probably worth thousands of dollars. So a $30 lunch definitely won't pay for their hourly rate.

That's why you should send a thank-you note their way.

In fact, a few months ago, someone invited *me* for lunch. And while they lived just a few minutes' walk away from me, they actually took the time out of their day to write and send me a thank-you card.

Handwritten notes don't happen all too often anymore.

That's why, if you write one, that note becomes very memorable.

For example, you just heard me recount a story of a handwritten thank-you note that someone sent to me a few months ago. I remember the handwritten note. I don't remember emails.

Your future mentor will probably be of a similar mindset.

And that's exactly what I did with my mentor. I sent him a thank-you note.

And honestly, I would not be where I am today without my mentor.

In fact, let's say that in an alternate reality, I *didn't* meet my mentor.

Here's where I would likely be without my mentor:
- An employee.
- Working 9 to 5.
- Chained to my work desk.

I would probably believe, still to this day, that I would be nowhere without the help of my boss.

But thankfully my mentor taught me to:

- Invest early.
- Think boldly.
- Think creatively.
- Build a business.
- Value relationships.
- Take calculated risks.
- Cultivate an entrepreneurial mindset.

These mindset shifts – and many others – helped me become the person I am today:

- Being free from the rat race.
- Earning passive income.
- Enjoying financial freedom.

And to be honest, not every mentor is the same.

Every mentor brings a different perspective and life experience.

That's why it's so important to first get to *know* your potential mentor first to see if you both actually "vibe," as they say today.

So, what if you don't have a mentor right now?

Well, that's probably why you're reading this chapter and book in the first place.

Here are the top three steps to building a relationship with a mentor:
- Identify a great mentor.
- Connect with a great mentor.
- Maintain a relationship with a great mentor.

Remember that if you want to become a winner – whether that's in your business, in your career, or in your life in general – you will have to think like a winner.

And if you want to think like a winner, then you'll have to surround yourself with winners.

Oftentimes, your future mentor is likely a winner.

And the right mentor will unlock your true potential within.

In life, there really are no shortcuts to success. Except mentors.

Mentors are the only true "shortcut" in life.

Mentors will:

- Guide you.
- Inspire you.
- Navigate you.
- Brainstorm with you.
- Ignite change within you.

The right mentoring relationship is a powerful way to thrive both personally and professionally.

Remember that because mentoring relationships are often informal and not rigidly structured with agendas, it might be tricky finding an "in" with a potential mentor. It might not be easy for someone to commit to mentoring you over the next few years.

That's why you'll likely have to actively seek out your mentors – such as by inviting them to lunch with you.

And, of course, it's worth noting that if you ask someone to be your mentor and they say "no," you should not take that as a personal rejection. It just may not have been the right time.

In fact, I would suggest for you to stay in touch with that person possibly once every quarter or every six months, by writing them an email, sharing any of your life updates, inviting them out to coffee, or simply sending them a "happy birthday" message.

Who knows? Maybe they will want to become your mentor down the road.

And this piece of advice flows directly into a key tip that I received once from my mentor:

Remember to maintain your relationships.

Have you ever heard that your network is your net worth?

That saying is 100% right – because your network can and probably will open doors for you that you probably didn't even know existed.

Alright, so let's get to the good stuff.

How do you *actually* find a mentor?

In the following, I'm going to share with you the five steps that I took to find my mentor – and 16 years later, I'm still in touch with my mentor, still learning from him, and still thriving from his advice.

How to Find a Mentor:

1. Research potential mentors who match your goals and personality.
2. Invite your potential mentor to a get-together for coffee/ tea or lunch.
3. Genuinely get to know them by asking thoughtful questions (without asking them immediately to be your mentor).
4. My best advice is to look for a mentor only if you are ready for a mentor.

In other words, don't force it. Because, trust me, they will notice and that won't necessarily look good on you.

Take the mentor search seriously because a mentorship relationship is like a lifelong friendship (mine so far is over 1.5 decades).

So take your time. You may not even find "the one" with your first try.

That's OK.

Don't forget to be picky when choosing your mentor either.

Because, trust me, your mentor will likely be picky in choosing their mentee as well.

Now that you know the five steps to choosing the right mentor, let's actually take some time to walk through each step.

How to Choose a Mentor

Step 1: Research potential mentors who match your goals and personality

Before you even start looking for a mentor, you should figure out *your* career and personal goals.

You want to know what *your* goals are *before* choosing a mentor because your mentor should have some sort of experience in the career or life that you want.

As an example, I knew I always wanted to:

- Become a leader.
- Build passive income.
- Run my own business.
- Increase my level of confidence.
- Think more boldly and creatively.

Back when I was a teenager, I did not have a lot of self-confidence.

Although I was very good at school and did have some leadership skills, I didn't exactly know how to apply my knowledge and I honestly had no idea which path to take in life.

I felt lost and needed guidance.

That's when I realized that I needed a mentor to help guide me.

However, before I started my mentor search, I wrote down the qualities and personality traits that I was looking for in a mentor.

Having a list helped me narrow my mentor search.

My goal was to meet a mentor who was:

- A successful entrepreneur.
- Someone who was kind and friendly.
- Someone who was a leader – not just a "boss."
- Someone who became successful because of their dedication and not their degree.

Now, it's your turn.

Take a pen to paper and list at least five things that you want in a mentor.

These things could be:

- Your mentor's goals.
- Your mentor's industry.
- Your mentor's personality.
- Your mentor's accomplishments.
- Your mentor's ability to communicate.

Speaking from personal experience, the best mentorship relationships are when you are both friends and trust each other.

Although a formal and more rigid mentorship can also certainly work in your favor, a mentorship that's more like a friendship typically sees more success.

That's because you'll likely receive more:

- Support.
- Feedback.
- Candid advice.

Typically, the more you and your mentor connect with each other, the more your mentor will be willing to help you out. For example, your mentor may connect you with their network, possibly even offering you a position in their company or business, etc.

Now, keep in mind that it will take *years* to build a solid mentor-mentee relationship. It took me 16 years and counting, so don't think your future mentor will offer you an executive-level position in their company by Day 2!

The other piece of advice I would offer is don't rush the mentor-mentee relationship.

If you rush the relationship, then it would probably be fake. Instead, let your connection with your mentor evolve and grow naturally. Building trust takes time.

Your mentor search may result in finding potential candidates from all types of backgrounds, such as:

- Your professors.
- Your family friends.
- Community leaders.
- Local business leaders.

Keep your eyes wide open because potential mentors are everywhere.

If you hyper-focus on one niche (such as just searching for local business leaders as your future mentor), then you might miss out on a great mentorship opportunity with someone else who might be a community leader, instead.

Step 2: Invite your potential mentor to a get-together for coffee/tea or lunch

Now that you've done your research on *who* your potential mentor(s) could be, the next step is to actually meet your mentor face-to-face (preferably) *before* you ask them to be your mentor.

I would *highly* recommend against asking someone to be your mentor without actually knowing them beforehand.

It's awkward, it's a bit strange, and it might not be the best base for a good relationship if you send a person a cold email, asking them to be your mentor – and they actually accept the request.

This scenario is like emailing a random person to be your best friend for life without even knowing that person.

So, find your potential mentor's email address, LinkedIn profile, and so on, and reach out to them.

The key here is doing something for *them* first (i.e., taking them out to coffee or lunch, e.g.). Don't ask them for anything in return – at least not during your first coffee or lunch together.

The reason why I suggest taking out your potential mentor for coffee or lunch is that coffee/lunch is typically informal, not too much money, and a small gesture.

I would typically recommend doing coffee if you don't know your potential mentor because coffee generally takes between 20 to 45 minutes, so you can leave the conversation faster if you don't like the person. Lunch on the other hand, will typically take a good hour or more.

Of course, if you already know your potential mentor from a previous interaction, then lunch may work just fine.

Here's how you can pitch coffee/lunch to your mentor:

- Connect with your mentor on a mutual interest.

For example, if you find out your mentor is on the board of a nonprofit organization that helps dogs – and you happen to be a major dog lover yourself – then you may want to reach out to your mentor saying something like this:

Hello XXX,

Your achievements in XYZ inspire me to become like you one day.

I also saw that you are a dog lover and help out on ABC Board. I am a dog person myself, having fostered two dogs and I adopted one of my own.

If you have a spare 15 minutes in your day, I would love to invite you out for a coffee/tea and get to know more about your passion as both a business owner and a champion for fostering animals.

Perhaps some of these times may work in favor of your schedule to meet at MNO coffee shop:

- **Time & Date 1**
- **Time & Date 2**
- **Time & Date 3**

Thank you for your time and I hope to meet you in person.
Respectfully,
WXYZ

I like giving my potential mentor three dates instead of just one, so they don't need to think of alternatives if one date/time does not work.

Make it as easy as possible for your potential mentor.

Another suggestion is to propose meeting your potential mentor close to where they work (so the chance they will agree to meeting you will be higher).

This means you may have to drive a bit farther to meet your potential mentor – but it may very well be worth the effort.

Just keep in mind that the easier you make life for your potential mentor, the more likely they'll agree to meet you.

Humans, in general, are drawn to the easiest option that requires the least amount of effort.

Step 3: Genuinely get to know your mentor by asking thoughtful questions

This is where you actually have the chance to get to know your would-be mentor!

Don't be nervous; this should be exciting!

Just remember to make a good first impression.

In fact, within the first seven seconds of meeting your potential mentor, you will make a first impression.[1]

It's not easy to change your first impression, either, after the first seven seconds have passed. In fact, many first impressions are lasting.

The following are some things that could impact your first impression with your would-be mentor:

- Your dress.
- Your posture.
- Your handshake.
- Your appearance.
- Your tone of voice
- Your body language.
- The pace of your voice.

Most importantly: Do not be late.

In fact, if I invite a mentor out to coffee/tea or lunch, I typically visit the area a day *before.*

I essentially pre-scout the area to make sure I:

- Know how to get there.
- Know which table to pick.
- Know the best parking spots.
- Know the menu beforehand.

One key tip that has worked for me is knowing *exactly* what menu item I plan to order before going into the coffee shop or restaurant. I don't want to waste precious time by browsing the menu when I could be talking to my mentor instead. So have a plan in place.

By visiting the site of your meeting before it actually happens, you're effectively preparing as much as possible.

You're doing your recon – just like any intelligence officer would as well.

And remember that as you are getting to know your mentor, **just be your authentic self.**

Otherwise, your mentorship relationship will likely be fake – and the last thing you want to be known as with your (potentially influential) mentor is a fake.

Remember this:

If your mentor doesn't like your personality, then the mentorship relationship was likely never meant to be. That's OK.

Keep looking.

Remember that you're not the only one who should be on their best behavior.

Although you want to make a good first impression, you should also keep an eye out to see whether your potential mentor makes a good first impression on you. . . . Remember that a mentorship relationship has to go both ways.

If you feel like something is off, then trust your gut.

That's why coffee/tea or lunch is such a great way to informally get to know someone – in a noncommittal manner.

Ideally, you'll want to keep your meeting short – between 15 to 60 minutes, maximum.

And once you have your coffee or lunch meeting with your mentor, I would also suggest coming prepared with a list of questions for them.

What's always worked for me was researching their LinkedIn profile, reading their bios, and maybe looking them up on social media to see if they have any common or shared interests. Of course, you don't want to come across as a "stalker," but at the same time, you do want to put your best foot forward and show that you've done your research and are genuinely interested in them as a person.

Come with a list of at least three questions to kick off the conversation, and then just go with the flow of where the discussion brings you.

You both might hit it off entirely or not at all.

That's the point of spending this time with them.

Step 4: Informally ask the person to be your mentor at a future date

After meeting your potential mentor, the next step you'll want to consider is:

- Whether you actually liked the person.
- Whether you think you'd be able to learn from them.

When I first met my mentor, I didn't immediately ask him to be my mentor.

I simply stayed in touch with him over the course of several months, meeting him and his wife at informal business engagements (and my parents also met my mentor and my mentor's wife).

During one of our informal meetings, it was actually *my mentor* who brought up the topic of becoming my mentor and helping me thrive in my career – I didn't even have to bring it up.

I realize that scenario might not be the case for everyone reading this book, but as you build trust over the long term, the likelihood of *them* bringing up mentoring you increases every day.

If you meet with your potential mentor over a longer period of time (like a few months), you'll allow your potential mentorship relationship to form naturally. That way, your potential mentor may actually be the one to bring up the topic of becoming your mentor versus you asking and potentially making things awkward.

I'm not saying that you *shouldn't* take it into your own hands.

What I am saying is that sometimes it might help to allow a little more time between your first meeting and when you ask them to be your mentor.

When you do ask for that person to be your mentor, I'd suggest for you to consider some of the following points:

- Be genuine in your ask.
- Mention what you specifically hope to gain out of your mentorship.
- Clearly suggest how many times, how long, and where you wish to meet your would-be mentor.
- Reiterate some key points that you remembered from your past conversations with your would-be mentor.
- Be specific as to *why* you want that person to be your mentor (e.g., bring up their accomplishments, their goals, passions, etc.).
- Give your potential mentor a way out – leave the door open in your ask so that your would-be mentor can say "no" without feeling uncomfortable or awkward.

Remember that even if they say "no" today, they may say "yes" in the future. So, if the answer is "no," then just stay in touch with them, reaching out every few months or so.

Maybe they are just too busy right now, but may possibly retire in a few years, freeing up their time, and they may want to take you as their new protégée.

You don't know what the future may hold, so accept the "no," but still stay in touch while you continue your mentor search.

And the best piece of advice I got from my mentor?

Never burn your bridges.

You never know if and when you may need to reconnect with someone who said "no."

Step 5: Meet and communicate with your mentor consistently

The next step of your mentorship has to do with meeting consistently.

Keep in mind that you will not achieve anything without consistency. It's virtually impossible.

So assuming your mentor agrees to help you on your professional and personal path, you'll want to establish a few things from the get-go:

- Where you want to meet.
- How often you want to meet.
- How long your meetings will last.

Since we live in post-COVID-19 times, meeting via ZOOM or other video calling services may be a good way to start. However, if you can, I would request to meet in person.

In pre-COVID-19 times, meeting in person would have likely been the best way to go.

My mentor and I have a good friendship, so I don't really send my mentor an agenda before we meet. We typically meet up at a restaurant for lunch or a coffee shop and simply dive into the conversation.

And the fun part is, I never know *where* the conversation will lead – but I always learn something new from my mentor.

For example, once I learned something about ceramic versus cast-iron race car brake disks! Another time, I learned about leadership assessment exams that my mentor used for his own employees (such as those used by Ray Dalio's behemoth hedge fund company to assess future leaders).

For those of you who don't necessarily know your mentor that well – yet – then it might be a good idea to prepare and send your mentor an agenda before your meeting.

The following are some tips you should keep in mind if you're planning to send an agenda:

- Send the agenda a few days to a week in advance.
- Send a few points on what you'd like to talk about during your meeting.
- Offer your mentor the chance to provide their thoughts on your agenda as well.

Once you're actually meeting your mentor, make sure to ask them for constructive feedback on your progress, your thought process, or any other area where you want to grow.

Ask your mentor to be as open and honest with you as possible – even if that means your ego may be harmed.

I'll give you an example of when my mentor didn't just deflate my ego, but pretty much popped my ego balloon and buried it in the ground . . . he was brutally honest with me and said that I was wasting my time in the job I was currently in. He said my job would not lead me anywhere close to my career goals.

Talk about a bracing and brutal reality check.

I wasn't prepared for that, but I'll tell you what, that conversation helped get me on track to where I really wanted to be: an entrepreneur, building my own business.

In the end, my mentor *was* right.

But not a *single* person in my network had the guts to tell me that what I was doing in my life was wrong – at least based on my aspirations and goals.

Either the people in my network didn't have the guts or they just didn't know.

Either way, that's exactly where my mentor filled that gap.

The path I had chosen at the time, which was being a 9-to-5 employee at a wealth management company, was *not* helping me in my career goals. In fact, it was taking me away from goal.

The feedback you get from your mentor might be *extremely* painful to hear (just like it was for me) . . . but let's be honest, you probably knew it all along, way in the back of your mind. You just didn't want to believe it and face it. The only difference is that your mentor actually told it to your face to make you change your trajectory for the better.

Keep in mind that the very reason why you *have* a mentor is to get life-changing feedback.

That feedback might not be all rainbows and butterflies, but mentors aren't there to give you happy and fluffy feedback. They are not supposed to be your best friend who says, "Everything will be OK."

Your mentor is there to give you a bracing reality check.

After every meeting with my mentor, I probably leave with 5 to 10 *pages* filled with information and notes.

Like I said, I learn so much every time I talk to my mentor.

That's why I would suggest you come prepared with a notebook and a pencil/pen to take notes, or you can record notes electronically using your laptop or record on your smart phone during your meetings with your mentor.

Now that you've established a solid mentorship relationship with *one* mentor, it might be worth considering establishing other mentor relationships.

Remember that one mentor will likely not be able to help you with *all* of your needs, which is why (just like with stocks), you need to diversify.

In this case, that means you may want to look into meeting people with *different* backgrounds.

Over the past decade or so, I've also had the opportunity to meet many diverse and incredible mentors.

The following is a list of my mentors:

- My mentor, the inventor.
- My mentor, the girl boss.
- My mentor, the Apple executive.
- My mentor, the college professor.
- My mentor, the serial entrepreneur.
- My mentor, the nonprofit executive.

Although I have mentors spanning across various industries and specialties, my main mentorship still goes back to my mentor who is the serial entrepreneur.

We just go back so many years and we stay in touch almost monthly. But that's completely normal – to have some mentorships that are stronger than others.

Before I close this chapter, I do want to list a few traits that you will (or should) find in high-quality mentors.

High-quality mentors are people who:

- Listen.
- Value education.
- Treat you with respect.
- Match your personality.
- Provide candid feedback.
- Are experienced in their field.
- Are passionate about helping you.
- Push you outside of your comfort zone.

Don't be discouraged if you don't find the right mentor immediately.

Like all good things, it may take time – and that's perfectly OK.

And whenever you *do* find the right mentorship relationship, it can literally transform your life.

It did for me.

Challenge #6: Find a High-Quality Mentor

Now it's your turn!

I just shared some of my *best* strategies and stories of my mentor. But it took me about 1.5 decades to get there.

If you haven't found your mentor yet – that's OK.

But now I want you to take some time to think about who the most influential and mentor-like people are in your life.

Do you already have a mentor?

If yes, do you think you would benefit from increasing the number of mentors you have?

Here are some points I want you to consider right now:

1. Write down your goals.
2. Research potential mentors.
3. Get to know your would-be mentor.
4. Informally ask the person to be your mentor.
5. Meet and communicate with them consistently.
6. Write down the people whom you would like to mentor you.
7. Reach out to your potential mentors and invite them to coffee/tea or lunch (in a public place) or to a one-on-one phone call.

Remember this

Although your potential mentor may have incredible achievements, it's also very important to keep up your guard. In other words, don't meet your would-be mentor in a private, nonpublic place. Always, always make sure to meet either publicly (like in a coffee/lunch shop) or via phone call or ZOOM meeting.

Although your mentor will probably be a "normal" person, you still *always* want to be on guard and protect yourself.

For example, let your parents, partners, and/or best friends know where and when you will be meeting with your potential mentor, just in case.

Never let your guard down.

The bottom line is that mentors are the only true shortcut to winning in life. When you find a high-quality mentor, you can learn from their mistakes and from their wins, which will help you save time, money, energy, and effort.

And now, go find your future mentor! If you do, send me an email and let me know how your journey went!

Note

1. Hinshaw, A. (5 Oct. 2020). Seven seconds to make a first impression –
Make it count! [online]. blog.thecenterforsalesstrategy.com. https://blog.
thecenterforsalesstrategy.com/seven-seconds-to-make-a-first-
impression#:~:text=Our%20brains%20make%20a%20thousand (accessed
2 July 2023).

Chapter 8

Stop Procrastinating

Do you know that I could have been $90,000 richer?

A *minimum* of $90,000 richer?

Yep.

I could have.

But I let $90,000 slide right through my fingers.

Imagine you have a big, fat stack of cash in front of you.

And all of sudden, you take that cash into your arms, and throw it into a metal trash can.

And then you decide to take a match, light it up, and throw the flaming match into the trash can with the cash.

You hear the crackling of the fire.

You see plumes of black smoke swirling toward you . . . and you realize that big, fat stack of cash is gone.

As if it never existed.

That's pretty much what happened to me when I missed out on $90,000.

At this point, you're probably wondering, *what the heck* actually happened??

And, my friend, it's a one-word answer.

Procrastination.

I procrastinated on starting my personal finance blog, The Millennial Money Woman.

In fact, I had the idea since 2016, but because I made too many excuses, was too lazy and too busy with all of life's little curveballs, I never got to building my website until 2020.

That's a whopping *four* years later.

Just imagine how much more money I would have made had I just started my website in 2016!

I mean I probably would have made a lot more than my estimated $90,000.

Since 2016, I always told myself that I would start my blog "tomorrow."

But then, I had an event the next day.

And the day after that, I was tired because I had a bad night's sleep.

And the day after that, I had to stay up late for work.

And so the days passed by . . . and I failed to stick to my goal of building my personal finance website.

That all changed when COVID-19 hit, and I knew I had to do something to help at least a few of the 16.9 million people who lost their jobs due to COVID!

And that was my sign to start buckling down on my dream and make it a reality.

That took me four years.

And a pandemic to get started!

Hopefully you can learn from my story and make that jump today. In fact, if you're reading this and always wanted to do something (whether start a business or side hustle, e.g.), then *this* is your calling.

This is your signal to actually start and go do that thing.

Don't be like me.

Don't procrastinate for *four* years and lose *thousands* of dollars in the process.

But then again, procrastination is pretty normal.

In fact, have you ever found yourself procrastinating?

Chances are, you have – and procrastinating is actually a pretty normal thing to do.

And quite honestly, it's no wonder that both you and I are struggling with procrastination since there is:
- Too much information.
- Too much negative news.
- Too many advertisements.

The truth is, procrastination can seriously slow you down.

In fact, 88% of workers admit they procrastinate for a minimum of one hour a day.[1]

If you are worried that you're the only person in the world who seems to be putting things off into the future, you are not alone.

If you're a college student, it's even more common.

In fact, 80% to 95% of college students have been found to procrastinate, according to research from the University of Calgary.[2]

So, as you can see, procrastination is a widespread issue.

I procrastinated for years before starting my personal finance platform and community.

Since then, my platform has helped millions of people better understand money, get out of debt, and work toward the life that they've always wanted to live.

Now, I'm at the point where I think "what could have been had I started four years earlier."

Who knows where I would have been had I started earlier. So, don't be like me and procrastinate for four full years.

Becoming your own boss, which is what happened to me when I finally decided to stop procrastinating, is one of the best ways to make money, help people, and live life on your own terms.

What's not to like about that?

Of course, running your own business may sound idyllic . . . but, trust me, it's not.

At least not at the start, which is probably the hardest because it takes SO much effort (I probably worked over 120 hours a week) and you get paid $0 for at least the first 6 to 9 months.

If I had to do it again, though, I would.

Now, it's your turn.

I want *you* to think about a life project that you've always wanted to do, but have been putting off. Procrastinating. Just like me.

This "life project" could be:

- Starting a blog.
- Writing a book.
- Starting a business
- Traveling the world.
- Repairing the house.
- Starting a nonprofit.
- Becoming an influencer.

It really could be anything.

Think about where you would be if you didn't procrastinate.

Think about how your life could have changed – for the better or worse – had you started your dream life project earlier.

If you want to learn how to start breaking through procrastination barriers and start working toward your goals, this chapter is meant for you.

***

According to Joseph Ferrari,[3] a well-known psychology professor at DePaul University, there are three main reasons why most people procrastinate.

Those reasons could include:
- You can't make a decision.
- You want to avoid a stressful subject at hand.
- You desire an adrenaline rush by working against the deadline.

And, procrastination can lead to increased levels of:
- Stress.
- Fatigue.

- Anxiety.
- Depression.

The good news is that there is a way to fix it.

And in this chapter, I'm going to share with you exactly what needs to be done in order to fix your case of procrastination.

According to Mel Robbins, a TEDx speaker, television host, author, and accomplished reporter, procrastination is actually a way to relieve stress.[4]

In fact, Mel suggests that procrastination is a defense mechanism that humans have built to battle life stress.

That stress could be related to:

- Work.
- Financial.
- Relationship.

For example, maybe you work for a boss who is a really mean lady (this actually happened to me in the past).

Maybe this woman never says anything nice to you (not even a thank you, as was my case), and only gives you the hardest projects. And if you miss the slightest detail, then this boss calls you out on this detail.

Sound like fun?

It didn't to me either, and that's why I *always* left this woman's projects to the very last minute.

In fact, every time I received an email from her, I had a little heart palpitation!

It made me nervous just opening her emails because I knew she was going to make some silly request that would take hours of my time. So I left her emails unread to the last minute.

That is an example of procrastination in my life because of work-related stress.

Think about a time when you encountered stress. Did you cope by procrastinating?

In fact, if you were like me, then procrastination may have actually become a habit. In other words, leaving your boss's email unread until the last minute would become a subconscious habit. You wouldn't even have to think about it anymore.

And if you are familiar with the components of a habit, you'll likely remember that there are three things that make up a habit:

- Trigger
- Pattern
- Reward

Let's explore these three components of the procrastination habit a bit further.

Component	The Procrastination Habit
Trigger	Life stress
Pattern	Procrastination – you avoid doing something
Reward	Temporary stress relief

Take a look at the row titled "Reward."

Do you see how procrastination is essentially a *temporary* form of stress relief?

Going back to my example, whenever I procrastinated and refused to open the emails from my mean boss, I gave myself a temporary stress relief because I didn't know which task to complete.

Now, the key word here is that procrastination is only a *temporary* form of stress relief.

That's because if you are stressed and don't want to do a stressful activity, you resort to procrastination. However, the fact that you procrastinated will make you even *more* stressed out about completing that particular activity, leading to potentially more anxiety and stress.

So, as I see it, procrastination is really a downward spiral – it's vicious and you really need to learn how to stop procrastinating.

The sad truth is that you'll probably never get rid of the stress in your life.

You'll probably always face some type of stress – whether that's about relationships, money, or work – but the good news is that you can change your current pattern of procrastination when you are stressed.

Mel Robbins suggests a few tricks on how you can replace the procrastination pattern with something productive, like taking action.

Steps to break procrastination:
- Acknowledge the stress you're facing.
- Slowly start counting backward for five seconds.
- Begin working on the stressful subject for just five minutes.

The reason why these three steps are so effective is because when you start pursuing an activity, it is human nature to continue with that particular activity for more than just five minutes.

So you are essentially trying to psychologically trick yourself by saying you are going to tackle an activity for just five minutes, when in reality, you'll probably keep working on that activity for more than five minutes.

And remember that everyone, no matter if you're the wealthiest or poorest person in the world, only has 24 hours each day.

That means:

- Your time is limited.
- Stop overthinking.
- Start doing.

One tip that has tremendously helped me cut back on my procrastination and move closer toward my goals, goes back to the very first chapter of this book: **Finding your purpose.**

Make sure everything you say, everything you believe, and everything you do is aligned.

Align your actions with your words.

You cannot live a happy and fulfilling life (or at least, it will be pretty difficult) if you do something or work in a career that does not align with your beliefs.

Here are a few tips that can help you cut down on procrastination:
- Set multiple, evenly spaced deadlines.
- Understand how you operate best.
- Surround yourself with winners.
- Connect with your purpose.
- Maintain a clear vision.
- Pay it forward.

Let's break down these steps into actionable items.

How to Cut Procrastination

Step 1: Set multiple, evenly spaced deadlines

First, and I think most importantly, an easy way to crush procrastination is to set multiple, evenly spaced deadlines.

So let's say your goal is to open a business.

That's a pretty big goal . . . and it's a bit daunting, if you ask me, because most people who have never started a business before typically don't even know *where* to start.

So having a goal that states "open a business" is pretty vague and pretty scary to most people.

However, you can overcome procrastination by breaking down your big goal (opening a business) into many smaller tasks/goals with evenly spaced deadlines.

Here is an example of the two scenarios:

One Big Goal:	Open a Business in six months.

While this is a fantastic goal to have – opening a business – it's still pretty scary because there is zero clarity around *how* to actually open a business.

It is one single deadline and one seriously scary project.

Now, let's see how this one goal could be broken down into smaller, more actionable tasks/goals with evenly spaced deadlines (keep in mind, this is just an example).

Goal	Deadline
Brainstorm business ideas.	June 1
Shadow industry experts to become familiar with the business.	June 15
Do your business research.	June 29
Interview potential customers to figure out their pain points.	July 13
Research country and/or state laws to make sure your business complies with them.	July 27
Consider titling your business as an LLC or other type of business entity.	August 10
Determine if you need to secure financing.	August 24
Research your competitors.	September 7
Research barriers to entry.	September 21
Develop a business plan.	October 5
Network in your local community.	October 19
Request for mentors or local community leaders to join your business "advisory board" (if you have one).	November 2
Research a potential marketing or media campaign.	November 16
Begin building out your product line and/or services.	November 30
Make any final business preparations.	December 14
Open for business.	December 28

What was your first thought when reading this list?

Maybe you thought it was overwhelming (I did).

But when you compare *this* list with actionable items versus the original task of just "open a business," I'd honestly say that evenly spaced deadlines is much easier to digest because it gives you a clear roadmap of what you actually have to do and when you have to do it.

When I see the second chart, I feel like I can make my dream of opening a business a reality.

When I see the first chart, with the goal of simply opening a business, I feel heart palpitations because I am filled with anxiety: I don't even know where to start.

And that first point goes back to the feeling of anxiety.

If I have a very vague task at hand, I become anxious, which then makes me want to avoid tackling the project because I don't have clarity.

And that's how procrastination starts.

So, the very first step to crush procrastination is by creating very clear, very specific step-by-step actionable tasks so you know *exactly* what to do and *when* it has to be done.

Step 2: Understand how you operate best

As you know, every person works differently.

Some people work well in the following environments:
- Fast-paced
- High-stress
- High-pressure

On the other hand, there are some people who work really well in the opposite type of environment:
- Slow-paced
- Low-stress
- Low-pressure

In which type of environment do you thrive?

To work efficiently and effectively – and to cut out procrastination from your life – you want to make sure you understand how you best perform tasks.

Put yourself into a power position where you optimize your strengths to complete the tasks at hand. That's when you get the opportunity to cut out procrastination.

Think about this example:

If you work best in a low-pressure and low-stress environment, would you still work at your best level in a high-pressure and high-stress situation?

The answer is probably not.

Make sure you understand how you best operate to extract your optimal performance.

If you aren't sure how you best operate, then I'd suggest experimenting with different work conditions and take note of how you react and whether you thrive.

And remember to stay true to yourself when you evaluate how you best operate.

Step 3: Surround yourself with winners

Your environment, in part, will determine whether you thrive or whither.

Here's a perfect example:

If you put a shark, arguably the king of the ocean, on land, the shark will not survive.

That doesn't mean the shark is weak.

It just means that the shark is in the wrong environment. It can't thrive. And it can't win if it is put on land because the shark dominates the water and not the air.

Similarly, you have to make sure that your environment gives you the elements that you need to thrive – not just survive.

Do you already know which environment gives you the best winning chance?

If not, that's OK – it may take years to understand how you best operate.

But it is your job to create the environment that is best for you. So the earlier you find out, the better.

Trust me, don't wait for your boss to ask you which environment you would need to survive and thrive.

Your boss will probably not take the time, energy, or money to help build the environment you need to thrive.

And that's why this part is up to you.

From my experience, you get the highest chance of success when you surround yourself in an environment with winners and people who are better than you.

Yes, I know it can be intimidating if you're essentially the least knowledgeable person in the room – but imagine just *how much* information you will learn!

In fact, have you ever heard of the saying by Confucius:

"If you are the smartest person in the room, then you are in the wrong room."

It's true – life is a never-ending journey of learning.

And if you want to be a winner, you have to think like a winner, which is why you should surround yourself with winners.

Step 4: Connect with your purpose

One of the fastest ways to crush procrastination is when you do what you love.

Now, the first time I heard this advice, I brushed it off. I thought it was some sort of cliché advice that was given to young college graduates and didn't think a second about it.

But. You know who gave me that advice?

One of the vice presidents of JPMorgan and Stanley. Yep. A company that is worth $354.4 billion. That's *billion*.

So I should have probably listened to this vice president, don't you think?

And think about it: Why would you put off doing something when you enjoy it? When you love it?

That's why it's so important to understand your purpose (reread Chapter 2 if you want a refresher).

When you connect with your deeper purpose, then in a way, you connect your mind with your heart.

And when you connect your mind with your heart, you will become unstoppable.

Let's take my situation as an example:

I am a personal finance blogger.

I decided to share my financial knowledge and experience with millions of people around the world because I know firsthand what it is like to *not* understand money.

I've lived through the harsh reality of being poor. I slept on a mattress made out of towels for crying out loud because I didn't have enough money to afford an actual spring mattress!

I know what it is like having to decide whether you should spend your last $5 on dog food for your pet dog or on Ramen Noodle Soup so you have food in your stomach for the night.

It was not fun.

And I felt absolutely helpless because I didn't know anything about money. And I was scared to even touch a financial book because I knew I would see hundreds of vocabulary words that I had no idea what they meant. It was all foreign jargon to me. A different language.

So instead of tackling my biggest fear – not knowing financial literacy – what did I do?

I procrastinated.

I decided to avoid the very thing that was giving me stress – not understanding basic financial concepts – which in turn, gave me more stress.

That all changed when I took some time to reflect on my situation.

I finally gathered the courage to pursue finance.

And so, many, many years later, my entire life is dedicated to helping other people understand personal finance. Why? Because I know what it's like to be in their shoes.

Helping others understand finance is my passion. It makes me feel like I'm doing something positive in this world – I'm helping people move one step closer to financial freedom.

And the reason why I'm so passionate about my work is because I can relate to everyone else out there who is stressed about money. I lived below the poverty line and know what it's like to worry every single day about money.

If I didn't connect my mind (my knowledge and experience in finance) with my heart (my passion to help others succeed financially), then I probably wouldn't have stuck through the tough time of being a financial blogger (working 120+ hours a week) and being paid $0!

When you include your heart (or your passion) in your journey, then you can virtually overcome anything:
- You will be more resilient.
- You will push through obstacles.
- You will be able to adapt to anything.
- You will thrive in the worst circumstances.

The key here is to connect your mind with your heart and you will thrive.

Step 5: Maintain a clear vision

In order to build the life you want, you first need to understand the type of life you want.

You can't build the life you want if you don't have a clear vision.

Here's how you create a clear vision:
- Know what you want.
- Visualize your future self.
- Picture how you feel in the future.

Then, you have to build the roadmap that will help you navigate the obstacles in life to help you arrive at your future vision.

It's very important to note that if your vision is vague, you probably will have a really difficult time achieving it.

Which vision is easier to accomplish?
- Vision 1: I want to be a millionaire.
- Vision 2: I want to have $1 million in my investments by the time I'm 65 years old.

The second statement is so much more specific and really makes you wonder, "OK, what's my next step to make this million-dollar dream a reality?"

From there, you can apply Step 1 to crushing procrastination, which is setting small and evenly spaced deadlines to accomplish your goal.

Here, you can build out the mini-steps you need to take in order to accomplish your goal of becoming a millionaire by age 65.

Step 6: Pay it forward

I am a big believer in giving back.

Although some may disagree, I strongly believe that giving back to your community and paying forward your success is such a vital life lesson.

After all, there is no such thing as "self-made." It takes an entire community.

Never forget who has helped you succeed along your path.

Once you feel that you have "made it," it's important to use your experience, knowledge, and expertise to positively help someone else's life.

My mentor taught me a valuable life lesson a long time ago:

When you give back, you will receive.

And he was right.

When you give back, you will find:
- Love.
- Gratitude.
- Happiness.
- Friendship.
- Community.
- Compassion.

And the best part about giving back is that you can actually see the positive impact you make.

Seeing the positive impact can bring you as much joy as the people who receive your gift!

There are three main ways you can give back.

You can give your:
- Time.
- Talent.
- Treasure.

You can donate your **time** by volunteering and *helping* wherever you may be needed.

You can donate your **talent** by teaching your *skills* and *knowledge* to those who may not have the resources to take classes.

You can donate your **treasure** by giving *money*.

Trust me, giving back will help you realize how lucky you are, and can, in fact, help you cut procrastination by connecting you closer to your purpose.

Challenge #7: Break through the Barrier of Procrastination

For this challenge, take some time to think about how procrastination has impacted your life.

Think about where you would be right now if you didn't put off doing those life tasks you've always wanted to accomplish (like opening a business, paying off debt, repairing the house, etc.).

Acknowledge that you've been procrastinating (if you have) and realize that you can make a change, starting today.

Here are the steps I want you to take:

1. Think about how you've been procrastinating.
2. Read through my steps on **how to stop procrastinating**.
3. Start your journey by setting small tasks/deadlines and working toward your goals.

Remember this

Procrastination happens to everyone – so you are definitely not alone. The great news is that you can make a change starting now.

Notes

1. Madiha-Hashmi. (2023). 30+ procrastination facts and statistics you were not aware of. Quidlo. Available at: https://www.quidlo.com/blog/procrastination-facts-and-statistics/#:~:text=Procrastination%20at%20Workplace,least%20an%20hour%20a%20day. (accessed: 02 September 2023).

2. Steel, P. (2007). The nature of procrastination: A meta-analytic and theoretical review of quintessential self-regulatory failure. *Psychological Bulletin*, *133*(1), 65–94. https://doi.org/10.1037/0033-2909.133.1.65.

3. Why do we procrastinate, and how can we stop? Experts have answers. (2021) *Washington Post*. Available at: https://www.washingtonpost.com/lifestyle/wellness/procrastinate-why-stop-advice/2021/07/09/13b7dc2c-e00e-11eb-9f54-7eee10b5fcd2_story.html (accessed: 26 August 2023).

4. YouTube. (2011, June 11). Available at: https://www.youtube.com/watch?v=Lp7E973zozc&t=1s (accessed: 26 August 2023).

Chapter 9
Embrace Failure

Back when I was a student in high school, I genuinely believed that the only thing to life was either failing or passing school.

I know . . . not the best way to view life, right?

In fact, I believed that whether you do good or bad in school would determine how your future life, after high school, would be.

Think back to your high school days.

Did you ever have a teacher that seemed like no matter what you did, you failed?

I had one just like that.

In fact, she was my 9th-grade English teacher. And no matter what I did, I could never make her happy.

In my 9th-grade English class, I had to sit in the very front row and literally in the dead center of the class. I sat right in front of where my teacher stood while teaching.

And the worst part?

Every time she said words that started with the letter "*p*" like "put the paper in the plastic pocket" she would unknowingly spit all over my desk. It was disgusting. I should have brought an umbrella to that class!

Whatever work I did or questions I asked in that class – it was never good enough for my teacher.

The worst part happened when I handed in my final English paper project. It was 10 pages long, and I had spent weeks working on that project. In fact, I had even asked an English teacher from the college near my house to review the paper with her suggestions, so I would have no room for error.

And you know what?

My high school English teacher gave me a grade that was just above failing.

Wow.

What an irony!

When I saw my 9th-grade English teacher hand back my almost-failing paper, I actually had to laugh. I had to laugh because it was in that moment that I realized the way I was living life – believing that how I do in high school will determine how I do the rest of my life – was completely and utterly wrong.

I realized that my belief was wrong because I had spent so much time and energy on that paper – and I even asked a well-known and respected college professor to check over my 9th-grade paper, who said it would have earned a top grade in her class.

And yet my 9th-grade English teacher didn't think so.

It was that moment when I realized I had to change my mindset.

Normally, I would have been very upset at the almost-failing grade I had received. I would have been dejected, not wanting to continue my studies.

But now my mindset was different.

Instead of feeling sad and fearing that my failure would negatively impact my life, I realized this was all part of the learning curve. It was all part of life.

It was that moment, sitting dead-center in the front of my English class that taught me a very important lesson: failure is never final. In fact, I learned that some people (like my 9th-grade English teacher) are *never* going to change. I also learned that I should not base my self-worth on what someone else thinks of me.

I learned to not base my self-worth off of external factors (like a grade that I *knew for a fact* I didn't deserve).

While this example might seem small to some of you, the experience taught me that failure is just a stepping stone to self-improvement.

Failure, I learned, is actually a very good thing to experience because failure actually gives you the chance to learn more about *who* you are and the type of *character* you have.

Originally, I thought the rest of life would be structured in a similar way to that of my school experience:

- Don't make mistakes.
- Always listen to one person (teacher).
- Never question what the teacher says.
- Always follow the rules without question.
- If you can memorize something, then you are smart.
- You receive instant feedback (in the form of your grades).

Boy, was I wrong.

Looking back, I realized that I took everything I learned in school too seriously.

For example:

- I thought that mistakes were fatal.
- I thought that intelligence was based on grades.
- I thought that memorization was the key to intelligence.
- I thought that teachers were always right, no matter the circumstance.
- I thought that doing poorly in school meant you had no chance for a successful life.

Did you ever believe some of these points? Which ones?

When you are in school, you probably don't know better because you haven't had the chance to experience life yet. But now, many years after graduating high school, I can see how wrong I was.

Unfortunately, many more of us erroneously believe these thoughts as well. And the way that most of us were taught and brought up in our school system, sadly, was not in our favor.

We were taught to:

- Avoid critical thinking.
- Become great employees.
- Avoid talking about finance.

The most fatal flaw of my high school experience was learning that failure and making mistakes was a bad thing. As an example, every time we made a mistake, we received immediate, negative reinforcement (like a bad grade, staying after school for detention, the teacher yelling at you in front of everyone in class, etc.).

In fact, I once read a blog article that compared the school system to the prison system. . . .

In school I was *so* scared of making a single mistake that I lost my creativity, I lost my spark to think critically, and worst of all, I lost my passion for trying new things because I was too afraid to fail.

School taught me that failure is fatal.

In the words of Nelson Mandela,

"I never lose. I either win or learn."

Now that's a winning mindset.

That's the mindset you need to overcome fear of failure because, in the end, fearing failure is the same as fearing success.

And, sadly, schools teach us that mistakes are bad because we are punished regularly for making them.

Yet, it is the natural human instinct to learn from mistakes – and that's why the rich often are not afraid of failure.

So let me tell you why most people never reach their full potential:

Most people allow fear to dictate their lives.

And when you live in constant fear of failure, you are, in a way, fulfilling your own prophecy. You are, effectively, failing by not reaching your full potential.

Have you ever heard of this saying by Vince Lombardi?

"Winners never quit. Quitters never win."

Over the past year, as I started building up my finance platform, The Millennial Money Woman, the true meaning of Vince Lombardi's saying became crystal clear to me.

I realized that those who get up after every failure, ultimately will win.

They don't care if they've failed 10 times.

Or 100 times.

Or 1,000 times.

Or 10,000 times.

They keep their eyes on their goal – whatever that goal is.

If you want to achieve your goals, you have to be willing to learn the lessons taught by your failures.

If you want to win, then you cannot quit until your dream becomes reality.

So, for example, back in 2020 I started my personal finance platform, The Millennial Money Woman. In fact, I started my journey alongside about 34 other people, who also decided to build out their own personal finance platforms in 2020 when COVID-19 hit.

I never quit and am still running my platform, almost four years later.

My first one to two years were extremely difficult. You don't know how many times I wanted to quit because I didn't see results. I wasn't making money and I was working over 100 hours a week. For no monetary reward.

But because I was disciplined, I stuck with it.

Even when my motivation faded, I woke up every morning at 5 a.m. (sometimes even earlier!), I meditated for 10 minutes, and then I jumped into my work.

I ate so poorly (living off of Ramen noodle soup virtually every lunch) and worked so many hours that I felt like I had a permanent cold. But I never stopped my mission.

My mission was to help others build a better financial life.

And you know what?

I failed SO many times.

Countless times.

For example, when I first started building my business, I thought that all I needed was to build a website to help people. But I was wrong.

While my website did do pretty well after about 14 months (I was earning between $5,000 and $9,000 per month in purely passive income from affiliate marketing), Google changed its algorithm. And the algorithm change hurt every small website and small business owner while generally benefiting larger websites.

This algorithmic change hurt my website's visibility (since my website was not ranking high on Google search results), and ultimately not many people read my content.

So, I had to pivot.

I still kept adding content to my website, but also shifted focus to building a social media presence. I realized that if I wanted to keep my platform alive and continue boosting its social presence, Google alone would not do the trick. I would have to create a social media presence as well and advertise my platform on social media.

My first step was Pinterest because I observed that other prominent personal finance creators used Pinterest.

And while the Pinterest social media platform did work for me for a while (I was reaching between 50,000 to 100,000 monthly views), the audience never really converted to readers. And then the Pinterest algorithm changed from one day to the next!

At that point, I knew I had to pivot again. And I took some time to research which social media platforms may do the trick. That's when I landed on Twitter (now X). Now, building a Twitter account was a pretty scary task because no other successful personal finance specialist had ever used Twitter as a full-time social media platform.

Instead, the more common platforms for successful personal finance content creators included Pinterest, Facebook, Instagram, and YouTube. So I was in brand-new, unchartered territory. But I was also willing to take the risk to commit some time and energy to X because I was new and really didn't have much to lose.

X worked.

If you haven't checked out my X profile yet, then you should. Within about two years, over 200,000 followers subscribed to my X profile, which was very humbling. But it took A LOT of work to say the least.

While I was building my website and my X presence in tandem, I realized that I wanted to continue building my presence online and keep helping people directly with their financial questions by providing live classes.

So I pivoted again.

Instead of just writing content for my social media platform (X) and my online platform (my website, The Millennial Money Woman), I also developed an online community.

Before I even committed the time, money, and energy to my community, however, I first did some boots-on-the-ground research. I wanted to figure out *what* my audience actually wanted to learn from me.

So I spent about 4 weeks, 30 days, nonstop connecting with my audience. I emailed them. I messaged them directly through the X direct messaging system. I jumped on short, 15-minute calls with my audience. I tried to understand as much as I could about where the majority of my audience is *right now* in the financial journey and *what it is* that they want to learn.

Those four weeks were very enlightening. I learned so much about my audience because I directly connected with them, one-on-one.

From that experience, I managed to group the majority of my audience's needs into three basic groups:

- Paying off high-interest credit card debt.
- Saving their first $1,000 for an emergency savings fund.
- Learning basic financial literacy concepts to help them build long-term wealth.

Using this information, I then started building my online community.

The online community, called Wealth Suite, took many months to plan before its launch. But, so far, that has been my pride and joy. Within just its first week, over 90 members signed up to join me during my live weekly calls and ask burning financial questions in the private community online channel.

I think the reason why the private online community worked so well was because many people *want* to get financial help from an experienced financial professional, but they don't want to pay the *cost* of that financial professional.

Well, with my community, which is a monthly recurring subscription model, I charge my members only $19 a month, which is less than a monthly premium Netflix subscription.

And you know what?

The community works. It's extremely gratifying talking with your audience one-on-one every single day and helping them get one step closer to their overall goal – whatever that may be.

The community itself is such a minor investment on my audience's behalf and the return on investment can truly be unlimited because I teach each and every member the exact wealth-building strategies I used to help millionaires make hundreds of thousands a month.

The success of the community has skyrocketed recently, and I expect it to generate recurring income of about $20,000 per month in the very near future.

I share this statistic not to boast, but to explain that you absolutely *can* make money – but with time.

There are so many people I know who dive head-first into an activity or side hustle, expecting to make $1,000 or even $10,000 a month by Week 2. And that's just not the case – unless your content goes viral for some reason. But getting viral content (at least from what I've seen) has a lot to do with luck. So don't count on it.

And if these people don't see any sort of positive cash flow within the first few weeks – or first few months – then they just give up. They stop pursuing their business or side hustle completely. Because there is no "money."

That's not the right mindset.

If you truly want to build long-term wealth, then you have to understand that good things (like making $20,000+ per month) take time. If anyone else tells you otherwise, they are lying or don't know better.

I failed many times.

I had to pivot many times.

And I probably will have to pivot again soon.

That's just the nature of being an entrepreneur.

While I never will feel like I have truly "made it," I know I've managed to get ahead of 97% of solopreneurs out there just because of one word: *persistence*.

I failed but I kept going.

I lost (a lot!) of money, but I kept at it.

These failures taught me many valuable life lessons, which I have condensed for you here:

- Persistence pays off.
- Consistency builds luck.
- Failures are learning opportunities.
- You cannot have success without failure.
- Success happens outside of your comfort zone.

To give you an example, back when I first launched my business in 2020, probably 30 other solopreneurs started alongside me, roughly at the same time.

However, building a business is tough. You get rejected pretty much ALL the time and you also don't always get fluffy, happy messages from your audience or customers.

In fact, my old college professor once told me that if you *don't* receive hate from your audience or competitors, you haven't made it yet.

And in some way, that's true.

Because, oftentimes, people who send you negative comments are very likely jealous of your success.

And how do most people react to someone else's success?

They try to put down that person by saying mean things or bad comments. They put that person down to make themselves feel better.

And yes, I've 100% been the target of multiple negative comments. And, trust me, it's not always easy to bounce back because, in the end, these comments do impact me.

But that's just part of the game as a business owner.

Not everyone is going to agree with you or like what you do – and that's OK because people are entitled to their own opinion.

It's your job – regardless if you own a business or are an employee – to build a tough skin. A solid outer shell to not allow those negative comments to penetrate your confidence or self-worth. Because, in the end, the people who reject you or say unfair things to you don't really know you. They don't know what you've been through. And they are honestly just what I call "keyboard warriors."

It's not an easy game, regardless if you have an online business or a brick-and-mortar business.

But, then again, if it was easy, then everyone would do it.

Circling back to the start of my journey where I – along with roughly 30 others – started my personal finance platform.

In the beginning, each and every one of us was excited to build our own, separate businesses.

We were working on it every single day.

And then the pandemic regulations slowly eased.

People started going back to the office and forgot about those side projects they once worked on, during the midst of the pandemic in early to mid-2020.

They started leaving their projects or businesses behind to get back to "real life." They stopped dreaming that they *could* actually set themselves free from the 9-to-5 grind and build their own financial empire. They left that behind.

And you know *the No. 1 reason* why they left that life behind?

They lacked consistency.

They thought that it would be *easy* to build a business and make money. To build long-term wealth. To pay off their debts.

Sadly, life isn't like that. Life doesn't give you the good stuff for free.

Ever heard of the saying "There's no such thing as a free lunch"?

Well, the saying has merit. There really is no such thing as a free lunch.

Now, about 3.5 years after I started building my platform, only three of us originals remain. That means 10% of the original solo-preneurs back in 2020 are still going. I mean, that's not bad, but it's not amazing either.

The others dropped off because:

- They went back to the office and neglected to continue building their business.
- They had life "get in the way," like having kids, and shifted their focus.
- They didn't want to work long hours with minimal reward.

And I get it; it's not easy *at all* to give *so* much time of your life – and give up time with friends, family, vacations, and so on – just to build a business that might or might not work out.

You always hear the success stories, right?

The underdog stories.

How someone went from rags to riches, right?

But for some reason, you never really hear the "average" stories or the "failure" stories. Why?

I think you can learn so much from the "average" stories or from the "failure" stories as well. They have so much detail and meaning that you can translate to whatever you're doing in life and hopefully take some nuggets of wisdom.

That's because failure is arguably one of our greatest life teachers – whether that's learning from our own failures or from someone else's failures.

In essence, you have to realize that failure and success are like yin and yang. They are part of a whole.

You cannot have success without failure.

And you cannot become successful in your comfort zone.

In fact, success is probably furthest away from your comfort zone. And that's why being comfortable with failure will push you closer toward success.

To become more comfortable with failure, start reframing your mindset. For example, instead of thinking that failure is bad, consider failure to be another word for *learning*.

You will never fail as long as you learn.

The only time you will fail is if you fail to learn.

Here's why failure works:

- Inspires growth.
- Promotes change.
- Teaches resilience.
- Redefines priorities.
- Improves perspective.

In fact, my mentor once said, "Rejection is redirection."

Failure simply helps you see what you didn't beforehand.

And my millionaire mentor taught me some very important lessons about *how* to fail. Yes, believe it or not, to have a *successful failure*, you need to learn the *right way* to fail.

Here's how to fail the "right way":

- Fail fast.
- Fail early.
- Fail often.
- Fail forward.

While the "average person" gives up after one failure, the true winners don't give up after the first failure. They simply redirect their energy. They pivot. And then they try again.

The winners understand that life is happening for them and not to them.

They recognize that with every mistake and with every failure, also comes a lesson and an opportunity to learn, build, and grow.

It is up to you to find that opportunity – even if it is disguised as hard work – and take it to grow and thrive.

So now the question begs: why do we see failure as something bad?

I saw failure as something bad because that's how I was taught in school: if I failed at something, the consequences were bad. For example, I got a bad grade, lower class rank, detention, public humiliation, and so on.

But the truth is that we shouldn't see failure as something bad or negative. This is where you need to reframe your mindset.

Failure is opportunity in disguise.

So, let me ask you this: do you want to be successful?

If you answered "yes," then you must know that to be successful at anything, whether that's becoming the best plumber or the best business owner in the world, you must become comfortable with failure.

Don't believe me yet?

OK, let's talk about another real-world scenario about a company you most definitely know: Amazon.

What's one of Amazon's biggest successes?

Alexa.

Alexa is the voice-controlled virtual helper that can tell you anything from the weather to your shopping list. If you connect it correctly, then you can even ask Alexa to turn off the lights in your house, increase the heat by one degree or play a certain song.

Yes, Alexa is *that* advanced.

In fact, Alexa has become such a trailblazing icon that companies like Google and Apple have also tried building such advanced voice assistants like Alexa.

Before Alexa was created, however, things looked a little more bleak, a little less exciting. Let me explain.

Jeff Bezos, founder of Amazon, was starting a new project: developing the Fire Phone.

Ever heard of it?

Me neither. And that's probably because the Fire Phone was one of Amazon's worst and most embarrassing failures.

Launched in 2014, the Fire Phone was the first smartphone of its kind to offer customers the ability to scan barcodes on products they found while shopping. Once scanned, the phone would then give customers the opportunity to buy the product on Amazon (for presumably a cheaper price).

It sounds like an interesting vision . . . but the project failed – miserably.

The Fire Phone cost a lot of money, didn't really have the same great software as the Apple iPhone did at the time, for example, and it also had an exclusive contract with AT&T, which didn't exactly help broaden its reach.

Yet . . . Jeff and his team learned from their failure with the Fire Phone, which led to one of Amazon's greatest developments: Alexa.

Even billionaires who have more resources than what you and I can ever dream of in our lifetimes can and do fail.

Jeff Bezos probably had the smartest, best people working on his Fire Phone project, and yet they failed. But they managed to turn that failure into a learning lesson, and use their newfound knowledge to spearhead the Alexa project.

You cannot win unless you dare to fail.

Here's a quote from Jeff Bezos himself:

"The whole point of moving things forward is that you run into problems, failures, things that don't work. You need to back up and try again."

Trying again. That's the key.

Let's dissect another example of failure leading to success.

Take one of the world's most famous dreamers: Walt Disney.

Walt Disney invented the following:

- The theme park.
- The multiplane camera.
- The first full-length animated film.
- Cartoons with synchronized sound.
- Cartoon culture icons like Mickey Mouse.

Yet, Walt Disney experienced failure early on – when he was just 17.

In fact, he was fired from his job working at a newspaper, *The Kansas City Star.*

And here's the ironic part: Walt Disney's boss, the editor, fired him because the editor thought that Walt "lacked imagination and had no good ideas."

That comment is almost comical because Walt Disney grew up to become one of the most famous creative dreamers in not just the country, but in literally the entire world.

Yet, in one of his first jobs, Walt was fired because his boss believed he lacked imagination.

Many of us today would consider that a failure – being fired from your job, right?

But not Walt Disney.

In fact, being fired from the newspaper was probably *the best* thing that ever happened to him.

Imagine if he wasn't fired. And if he had kept working at *The Kansas City Star.*

Maybe he would have never left. Maybe he would have kept working his way up the corporate ladder, never tapping into his gift of creating new things.

There would have been no Walt Disney World. There would have been no Disney theme parks in Florida and California. There would have been no Mickey Mouse cartoon characters.

But all of that did happen because of this failure. Because Walt was fired.

Being fired gave Walt a chance to re-create his world – and our world – as we know it today.

Still not convinced that failure is necessary to become successful?

Alright, let me share another story of failure about another famous guy whom you've probably heard of: Steve Jobs.

Steve Jobs is one of technology's most recognized creators.

He co-founded Apple and helped build it into a multibillion-dollar company.

Without Steve Jobs, there wouldn't be an Apple iPhone. There wouldn't be the Mac (with which this book was actually written!). And there wouldn't be Apple TV – just to name a few devices.

And you know what?

Steve *still* experienced failure. But he didn't let that failure stop him.

Unbelievably enough, Steve was fired from the very company he helped create: Apple.

But did he give up? Not a chance.

His very actions align with the quote, "rejection is redirection."

So, Steve Jobs redirected his career and founded another company:

- Pixar (a computer animation film studio).
- NeXT (a computer and software company).

Instead of feeling hopeless, Steve let the rejection fuel his spirit and passion to change the world. And he did it again by founding those two additional companies – *before* he was rehired by Apple!

His passion, purpose, and love for his work surpassed his fear of failure.

That's why Steve Jobs continued working, continued building, and continued succeeding.

And, ultimately, Steve Jobs was re-hired by Apple.

So keep this in mind as you start building your own path: When your passion for what you do outweighs your fear of failure, success will be waiting around the corner.

Once you finally lose your fear of failure, you will realize that the world will truly be your oyster.

Challenge #8: Embrace Failure and Conquer Your Fear

For this challenge, take some time to think about what you envision your future to be:

- Do you want to retire early?
- Do you want to run a nonprofit?
- Do you want to be a business owner?
- Do you want to quit your job but haven't taken the leap yet?

Now, take some time to think about why you *haven't* pursued your dreams.

What's holding you back?

Take a piece of paper and list the top three things that you feel are holding you back from achieving your future goals.

Chances are, fear is part of the reason why you have not accomplished your full potential. Maybe you fear being rejected if you apply to your dream job. Maybe you fear failing if you start a business.

This is the time to conquer your fear.

Here are your next steps:

1. Write down exactly and specifically what it is that you want to accomplish.
2. Write down what fears or doubts you may have.
3. Now think about whether those fears or doubts actually have merit.
4. Think about whether you would feel happier continuing your current lifestyle or whether you would feel happier living outside of your current comfort zone.

Remember this

What is worse than failure is knowing that you had a shot and simply didn't take it.

As the old saying by Wayne Gretzky goes: "You miss 100% of the shots you don't take."

Don't regret missing out on an opportunity. Take it, harness it, and learn from it, if you do fail.

In the end, without failure, there cannot be success. To embrace a winner's mentality, you must learn to unlearn what school has taught you for so many years: that mistakes are bad. Mistakes, in reality, are only a lesson to help you find your niche and your success.

Embrace your failure, learn from your failure, and build your success starting today.

Chapter 10

The Biggest Financial Decision of Your Life

What I'm about to share will undoubtedly be one of the – if not THE – biggest financial decision of your life.

So this is important, and you should listen up.

If you want to get rich, build wealth, and live the life you want – and deserve – then you *have* to understand that your future wealth is not just based on your own actions.

Nope.

Your future wealth is also based on how your *partner* treats money.

Your partner is the single largest financial decision of your life.

Now, I'm not suggesting here that the only way to become wealthy is by marrying a rich partner. Not at all. In fact, you can absolutely become wealthy even if your partner doesn't come from a rich family.

What it really comes down to is your partner's relationship with money.

For example, you may want to ask yourself if your partner:

- Is frugal with their money.
- Knows the value of a dollar.
- Spends every cent they make.
- Is interested in money matters.

For those of you who are shaking your heads or are not convinced that your partner is the single largest financial decision of your life, I suggest you continue reading this chapter – and then draw your own conclusion.

Although you obviously don't want your relationship with your partner to be like a business relationship, you do have to realize that your financial health also depends on your partner's spending habits, for example.

Think about it: You can't win if you're pulling one end of the rope and your partner is pulling the other end of the rope in the opposite direction.

As partners, you *both* should be pulling the *same* end of the rope, in the *same* direction, right?

You'll get there faster (wherever "there" is).

And the same goes for finance.

Let's say you're the frugal one. You care about your money, you don't spend much, you've paid off all of your debt, and you're saving and investing every spare cent you can find. That's all great and good – but it won't make a single difference if your partner is the opposite of you. If your partner spends every last cent they make.

If that's the case, then your partner, in essence, will be undoing *everything* you ever worked for. The many years of saving, investing, of giving up fancy vacations or fancy cars so that you can retire earlier. Your partner could undo *all* of that.

Do you really want that to happen?

The answer, obviously, is "no."

In fact, I really want to hit this fact home with you: that both you *and* your partner need to be heading in the *same* direction in order to win financially.

So, let me share a brief example of a former client I had. She was probably in her mid-twenties and making a six-figure salary, of which she invested a very large chunk every single year. She had a promising career and had built up a very nice nest egg since she first started working, which was at age 18.

In fact, this particular client was so frugal that she gave up a lot of life events like going out with her friends, going on a very well-deserved vacation, and so on.

She gave up a lot in order to build toward her future because she knew about the power of compounding interest (which is something that we will cover in a later chapter). She knew that building wealth started from a very early age, which is why she harnessed her twenties to save and invest as much as she could. That's why I was her wealth advisor, after all!

And then one day, my client introduced me to her boyfriend (now ex-boyfriend).

She wanted me to meet her boyfriend so that I could have more context when it came to planning their financial future together. And, yes, that meeting alone gave me a lot of context. It wasn't pretty.

After asking some probing questions to understand the boyfriend's background and relationship with money, I could have almost told you that they would not last. That's right. Because of money.

And here's why: her boyfriend had the YOLO (You Only Live Once) mindset.

Now, I get it; life is short and you never know when something might happen – but you also have to plan for your future. It's all about maintaining that healthy balance.

And her boyfriend took it to another level when it came to money.

Instead of saving at least a little bit, every single penny he earned was spent literally the same day. He would not even think about saving or investing for retirement.

And when I casually broached the topic about saving for retirement, he almost immediately replied saying that he doesn't believe in planning for the future. Fair enough.

My client's boyfriend was someone who owned a *very* expensive luxury car – one which cost more than what he made each year from his job.

So, after my first conversation with the two, and sensing that talking about money was a very sore subject with my client's boyfriend, I gave them some homework. I asked both of them to go out on a dinner date and create a family budget while they were on that dinner date together.

Several months after my initial meeting with both my client and her boyfriend, I asked her how their conversations were going when it came to money. I wanted to know if they had the chance to work on a budget together.

And my client almost broke down in tears. She said that things between them had become so strained that she's nervous just bringing up the *money* word. She let me know that her boyfriend did not want to discuss the budget with her and refuses to talk about any financial matters with her.

That's a pretty big red flag, at least in my opinion. While I counseled my client through the situation, it was not hard to guess that the relationship would likely not last – since money issues are one of the top three contributors to breakups or divorce.

And alas, after another few months, my client and her boyfriend were no longer together. The reason, according to my client? Money.

My client could not see herself with someone who was so financially irresponsible – and was so set in their ways without being open minded to new money management suggestions.

So before you consider spending the rest of your life with someone, you *really* want to make sure that your partner's attitude toward money matches your attitude toward money.

For example, your partner should:
- Support your financial decisions.
- Be willing to meet your goals halfway.
- Encourage you to spend below your means.

Your partner can make or break your future financial health and wealth.

Both you and your partner should be each other's accountability partner – making sure that both of you stick to your spending plan.

While it's always a bit harder to discipline yourself when it comes to spending, it's easier to stick to a budget if you have an accountability partner – such as your spouse – to help you stay on track and meet your goals.

As Benjamin Franklin once said, "Beware of little expenses; a small leak will sink a great ship."

And Franklin was right, because money issues are one of the leading reasons why marriages fall apart.

In fact, the likelihood of divorce increases to 45% when partners feel their spouses spend money foolishly.[1]

Even worse, couples that argue about money at least once per week are also typically 30% more likely to divorce in the future.[2]

As you can see, money plays a pretty crucial role in maintaining or separating relationships.

And if you are married and decide to divorce, a split could be *very* costly . . . the average cost of a divorce is around $15,000 per person, which includes attorney fees, tax advisor fees, etc. [3]

That's why it's so important to weigh the costs and benefits of finding, being, and staying with your partner.

Even if you don't decide to marry your partner, it is still important to ensure that you and your partner's financial goals are aligned.

So, my best piece of advice when you start to date someone is to make sure you pay attention to their spending habits.

And oftentimes, the small things give away your partner's biggest spending secrets.

Here are some things you may want to take note of:
- Does your partner rack up debt?
- Does your partner spend more than they earn?
- Does your partner treat their parents as an ATM?
- Does your partner seem to focus on (and buy) name brands?
- Does your partner live in the moment and not prepare for the future?

Of course, being with a person shouldn't *just* be focused about money. Relationships are so much more important than just money.

But, when the "honeymoon phase" is over and you start living in the real world again, you need be very sure that your partner can handle money the same way that you would handle money.

That's why it's important to pay attention to any red flags (like the ones previously mentioned) early in your relationship, before things get more complicated (like buying a house or a car together).

You will be SO far ahead, financially speaking, if you select a partner whom you love AND who is financially smart.

And by financially smart, I don't necessarily mean that your partner needs to have a finance degree focused in economics from Harvard University.

Not at all.

In fact, I think it's perfectly OK if your partner is *not* financially literate – not many people are, to be honest. The key is that your partner should be open and willing to *learn* about finance. That's really what counts.

And typically speaking, in most relationships you'll always have one person who is a little more financially literate than the other. That's perfectly normal and OK.

For example, I'm the one who *was* more financially literate than my husband – and that's simply because I had a formal education in finance and obtained my Master's Degree in Personal Financial Planning. I used to work in the wealth management industry, for crying out loud!

My husband, on the other hand, had a career in the military.

While he was very skilled in other areas, which I had NO idea about, he didn't really understand much about money when I first met him.

However, my husband was open (and eager) to learn about finance – and that meant the world to me. After reading some finance books (like *The Millionaire Mind* by Dr. Thomas J. Stanley) and other popular personal finance resources, and after asking many (too many!) financial questions, I would say that he is 100% financially literate.

In fact, I would argue that he knows more than some financial "gurus" out there!

A supportive partner is one who either is willing to learn or willing to teach about finance.

And that's what a successful relationship should be about – having a partner who is supportive, open to learn, and willing to grow together.

I think it's important to be open and honest about your finances with your partner – especially if you're planning for the long term.

Sadly, however, 40% of partners who are in serious relationships have committed financial infidelity by hiding checking accounts, savings accounts, credit cards, and so on from their partners.[4]

Although you may not be committing physical infidelity (aka cheating), committing financial infidelity can be as damaging – or even worse – than physical infidelity.

So, it's important for you to be honest with your partner – especially when it comes to your financial situation – as well as for your partner to be honest with you about their financial situation.

To help your partner open up about their financial situation, don't judge them.

Talking about money can be as intimate as being physically intimate with someone.

Even some of my old clients back when I was a wealth advisor were uncomfortable sharing their financial status – and I was their wealth advisor, so I had to know everything about their financial life!

Going into deep financial detail is like getting naked for the first time with your partner. It's awkward. It might be uncomfortable. You might be worried that they may judge you for whatever reason.

But it's very important to have "the talk" early on, so you know exactly what you're getting yourself into.

If you haven't yet had "the talk," then I'll share with you what my boyfriend-now-husband and I did to ease that weirdness so many years ago.

Coming from finance, I knew that a talk would be necessary if we wanted to move things forward in our relationship.

So I decided to invite him out to a nice dinner on a Friday evening. It was like a date night, but it did have an agenda (literally, I gave him an agenda!).

My goal was to list just four or five points that I wanted to discuss over dinner that evening.

Why dinner?

I know that talking about money – especially for people like my now-husband who didn't exactly have a finance background – can be a pretty intimidating topic.

Eating out at a nice restaurant, having a few drinks, and just having a casual chat about money can take the edge off the "money talk." Too many couples think that talking about money has to be in a formal setting, with notebook paper, pens, and calculators. That's not at all the case.

In fact, if you want the other person to open up about money, then you probably want to create an atmosphere that's inviting, friendly, casual, and fun.

And that's why I decided to make a reservation at his favorite restaurant.

Now, I do want to note here that I did not ambush him (that's never a good idea). Instead, I let him know *why* we were going to his favorite restaurant beforehand and I also gave him an agenda about a week before we actually went to the restaurant together.

I wanted to make sure he took some time to gather his thoughts before we started talking about money and our financial future together.

When the day arrived to have "the talk," it was SUPER chill!

We essentially laid our cards on the table and had an open conversation about our thoughts and concerns about money.

Now this was just the beginning of our future money talks.

We decided to schedule a date night money talk once every month at his favorite restaurant. Again, we tried to make the conversation fun but also helpful for both of us.

And that's something that I would encourage you to do as well – having a consistent schedule (maybe once a month or once every two months) where you and your partner talk about money.

It doesn't have to be at a restaurant; it can be at your house, too. But if you have the conversation at your house, I would suggest to also make the environment less intimidating. So, for example, you could pour yourselves a glass of wine, turn on some of your favorite (relaxing) music for background ambiance, and then maybe have some light appetizers on the side while you guys start talking about money.

The key here to building a strong money relationship with your partner is about having a judgment-free zone. That's the key.

Because if you (or your partner) judges the other, then chances are you probably won't open up about money any more in the future.

And in the end, it really comes down to finding a partner who is:

- Frugal.
- Like-minded.
- Supportive of your money habits.

I would encourage you to find someone with a winning – or at minimum an open – financial mindset.

Even if your partner isn't as financially literate as you, which is perfectly OK, it comes down to how you both support each other.

I'm very lucky my husband is eager to learn about money, participates (and sticks to) our family budget, follows the latest investment news, and invests whenever he can.

My husband is focused on our future together and he is dedicated to building our wealth together.

Together with your partner, you'll be far more successful than if you were alone.

One eye-opening statistic is that 86% of millionaires are married and/or have a partner.[5]

Why?

Because chances are, you'll probably accomplish your goal of building wealth twice as fast if you have two people working toward the same future.

It makes sense, too.

Your spouse or partner is the support system you will need to be financially successful – and two brains are always better than just one.

While love, of course, is a very important component to building a long-term and successful relationship with your partner, it's also very important to understand how your partner views money so you both can be successful in the future.

Challenge #9: The Search for "The One"

Take some time to read through this chapter and collect your thoughts about your current partner (if you have one) or your future partner.

Consider whether your partner would be supportive of your financial frugality (assuming you are the frugal one in the relationship).

Think about whether your current or future partner would be interested in learning more about money.

Can you actually see yourself moving ahead, financially, with your future partner or would they undo all of the financial work you've already done?

If you feel that your partner would not be supportive of your financial decisions, then it might be worth having an open discussion with your partner about your concerns.

Remember that your partner can either make or break your future wealth.

Here are some points you should start thinking about:

1. Your current partner.
2. Your financial goals.
3. Your current partner's financial habits and goals.
4. Whether you support your current partner's goals.
5. Whether your current partner supports your goals.
6. Whether your current partner's goals align with your goals.
7. Whether you are happy with the way things currently are or if you feel an open conversation with your current partner would be best to sort out your concerns and/or worries.

Remember this

It is important to openly and consistently discuss your current finances and your future financial goals with each other.

Notes

1. Wilkinson & Finkbeiner. (2018). Divorce statistics and facts: What affects divorce rates in the U.S.? [online]. Wilkinson & Finkbeiner, LLP. https://www.wf-lawyers.com/divorce-statistics-and-facts/ (accessed 4 July 2023).

2. Causes of Divorce. (12 April 2023). Divorce.com Blog. https://divorce.com/blog/causes-of-divorce/ (accessed 4 July 2023).

3. Williams, Geoff. (21 Dec. 2020). Cost breakdown of a divorce. [online]. *U.S. News & World Report* – Money. https://money.usnews.com/money/personal-finance/family-finance/articles/cost-breakdown-of-a-divorce#:~:text=Average%20Cost%20of%20a%20Divorce&text=Still%2C%20if%20you%20want%20a%2C%20estate%20appraisers%20and%20other%20experts (accessed 4 July 2023).

4. Passy, J. (21 Nov. 2021). Are you a financial cheater? Over 40% of Americans say they've deceived their partners about money. [online]. MarketWatch. Available at: https://www.marketwatch.com/story/are-you-a-financial-cheater-over-40-of-americans-say-theyve-deceived-their-partners-about-money-11637346867 (accessed 5 July 2023).

5. Hodge, Scott. (15 June 2012). Who are America's millionaires? [online]. Tax Foundation. https://taxfoundation.org/who-are-americas-millionaires/ (accessed 5 July 2023).

Chapter 11

Increase Your Millionaire Odds

B elieve it or not, your chances of becoming a millionaire (or at least significantly more wealthy than you already are) can be increased by A LOT if you do one specific thing.

Interested?

Keep reading because, in this chapter, I'm going to share *exactly* the advice I received from my millionaire mentor that made me over six-figures in less than two years.

In fact, if my mentor didn't take the time to share his life experience and advice with me, I don't know where I would be today.

One rainy spring morning, during our quarterly meetings, my mentor shared this valuable information with me. We met in a corner café located in the middle of a big, metropolitan city, with cars and buses honking at each other so often that it almost seemed like a background song in a movie.

We were tucked away in the corner of the café, where I had laid out my notebook and some pages with questions I had prepared for our conversation.

For some reason, my mentor really enjoyed sharing his life stories over coffee or tea and croissants, and I didn't mind that either.

And it was during that rainy morning that he gave me the life changing advice:

If your goal is to become financially free, then you have to bet on yourself.

In other words, you have to become your own boss.

My mentor shared this golden nugget with me, back when I was 16 and still in high school, just about to graduate 10th grade and enter my junior year.

He told me that he learned this lesson from a very early age – in his mid-twenties – when he realized that being an employee will almost always keep you tied to a boss or a business that dictates your growth rate. But being a business owner, an entrepreneur, can give you unlimited income growth.

I countered my mentor by asking, "What if your business fails?"

To that, my mentor chuckled and swiftly replied, "If your business fails, and granted, there is a pretty high chance that within the first five years the majority of start-ups will fail, then you have this amazing experience and set of skills that you can use for a future job, if that's what you want. No one can *ever* take that solopreneurship experience away from you."

I nodded.

If you build your own business, and let's say that it does fail, no one can ever take that experience away from you. Business owners in general are a different breed; they are self-starters; they have dedication; they are typically good at time management; and they are disciplined. These are all vital skills you need to be successful – whether that's building a company on your own or being a top performing employee.

While my mentor's advice echoed in my mind, I sadly did not take that advice to heart – at least not for the next nine years. Instead, I took the traditional path.

First, I completed high school in America and then I went to college where I:

- Studied.
- Memorized.

- Regurgitated lessons.
- Wrote essays about biology.
- Learned about poetry studies.

And let me tell you, the classes – even those offered in universities – still don't prepare you for what lies ahead in real life. I should have known better.

Here are some of my regrets when I was in my early to mid-twenties:

- I *wish* I had learned how to build my own business.
- I *wish* I hadn't poured 100% of my time into school, memorizing facts.
- I *wish* I had taken time to network with entrepreneurs and business professionals.

By sticking so rigidly to an academic curriculum, I missed out on an essential part of life: gathering experience.

And the only way you can gather experience is by living *outside* of the classroom, meeting people, and learning hands-on what works and what doesn't work for you.

Instead, I did the opposite.

I studied and followed the academic curriculum. And so, the university continued teaching me:

- That mistakes are bad.
- How to follow the crowd.
- How to be a great employee.
- The definition of covalent bonds.

Looking back on my experience, I realized that school teaches you to become a great employee. But it doesn't give you the tools to become a great business owner – at least not most schools.

And I fell for that trap – initially – even though my mentor had warned me back when I was 16 years old. He had told me the secret to maximizing my chances of becoming wealthy.

So if your ultimate goal is to break free from the rat race, then your best bet is to build your own business.

In fact, 88% of millionaires are wealthy because they are business owners and entrepreneurs.[1]

I should also clarify that none of these millionaires were given an inheritance from their families. They had to work hard on their own to build their wealth.

In fact, only 3% of millionaires received an inheritance at or above $1 million![2]

I think it's so important to mention these statistics because there are A LOT of naysayers out there. People who just don't want to credit millionaires for their own hard work. People who hastily jump to conclusions and say that the majority of millionaires have so much money because they inherited it.

That's just absolutely not the case.

In fact, as a former wealth advisor, I can also share a little bit of background information on that mistaken belief. Out of the 453 millionaires with whom I worked, I would say less than 2% of them came from wealthy families originally.

Virtually all of them had to work hard in the beginning to build up their wealth. And, yes, most of the millionaires I worked with were, in fact, business owners.

One of my former millionaire clients who was probably worth about $40 million, for example, was a famous real estate developer in New York and Florida. I met him and his wife when they were about 70 years old and they had more money than they could ever spend. But you know what fascinated me about his story?

This deca-millionaire started his career as a newspaper carrier out of all jobs! Originally, his parents believed he would be living with them for his entire life. But this person found his love and passion for real estate and made some very shrewd deals before land prices in New York City shot through the roof.

While this millionaire was not "book smart," as some say, he was "street smart."

And it's *very* important to have street smarts – arguably more so than book smarts.

So, if most millionaires today did not inherit their wealth, then how did they make so much money?

The simple answer is a four-letter word: Grit.

Let me take you back to my conversation with my mentor, at the bakery, from Chapter 2.

Here are some quick facts to jog your memory:

- At 24, he was fired from his first real job after working there for just two years.
- At 26, he started his first business, and failed, going bankrupt.
- At 29, he started his second business, selling health insurance to businesses and sold that business for tens of millions many years later.

As you can see, my mentor was *not* a good employee.

And, not surprisingly, my mentor was only an average student at school. In fact, he would argue he probably was worse than average at school.

And my mentor most *definitely* did not come from a wealthy family – or let alone from a middle class family. He grew up without a father. He and his mother lived in one of the poorest – and probably one of the most violent – parts of town. But against all odds, my mentor made it.

My mentor went against the mainstream. He went against the crowd.

So his answer really shouldn't have surprised me when I asked him the following question.

When I was about to turn 18, I asked my mentor about his college career path and whether he would recommend that I apply for a prestigious Ivy League college and spend $100,000s in student loans or whether I should try to keep my college expenses at a minimum.

Once again, my mentor chuckled at me and shook his head, answering "no."

It was my mentor's opinion that spending hundreds of thousands of dollars on an Ivy League – or other private university – would not necessarily be worth the cost and debt.

Here's what my mentor said, "I know people who went to a local community college, got a degree in Liberal Arts and then went on to build their multimillion-dollar business. Heck, I even know a few people who dropped out of high school to start their own company and they are now wealthier than I am!"

Oftentimes, I feel like school and society in general creates these strict rules to follow. First high school, then college, then a job, then retirement, and so on.

But my mentor goes against all of the conventional ideals.

Instead, he follows his heart and seeks out a new path, like building a business when all of the odds are against him.

And clearly his mindset does work.

Here are my mentor's achievements:
- Owns 21+ businesses.
- Owns his own private jet line.
- Is a deca-millionaire ($10 million+).

While you and I are just seeing the tip of the iceberg with my mentor living a luxurious lifestyle, it certainly wasn't always good times. Especially not during the building and growing phase.

Here is how my mentor accomplished his successes:
- Grew up without a father.
- Went to a public state school.
- Almost failed out of high school.
- Studied liberal arts in college.
- Grew up in the worst neighborhood.
- Was fired from his first job at age 24.
- Absolutely hated working for others.

My mentor was impatient; he hated taking orders from bosses, and he felt like his true potential was being held back by his boss.

Working for someone else failed to spark my mentor's passion. And he felt miserable.

So, at one point, my mentor just didn't care anymore – and that's why he was fired from his first job.

Was he sad? Absolutely not.

In fact, my mentor was *relieved* that he was fired because now he could dedicate his time to his passion and purpose (read Chapter 2 if you want to learn how to find your purpose).

His purpose was to help protect families from suffering financial ruin caused by medical bills. So, my mentor started selling health insurance first to individual families and then to business owners.

And the rest is pretty much history.

Wealth Lessons

Over the past roughly 15 years, I've had the opportunity to listen to countless hours of invaluable information from my mentor.

It was a tough undertaking, but I wanted to condense the four most valuable pieces of advice I learned from my mentor for you.

Let's dive right in.

Lesson 1: The rich aren't employees for long

My mentor taught me that to be rich – to truly build wealth for the long run – your best bet is to build a business.

Of course you can build wealth by being an employee too (you can be a lawyer, doctor, engineer, financial professional, teacher, etc.). The key is just not spending as much as you earn.

And arguably, not every millionaire started out as a business owner right after school. Many millionaires – like my mentor – spent some amount of time being an employee. Being an employee gives you certain benefits, too.

For example, you can learn a little about yourself (like whether you like being a job holder or a job provider), or whether you even like the industry that you are in. My mentor viewed his time as an employee as a learning experience. Being an employee can also teach you valuable skills from your superiors and these skills can give you a head start when you build your business.

So being an employee is not all bad. But, if you are an employee, you still are working for someone else. Your schedule and your income is based on someone else's agenda. Not yours.

To become rich, you need to hire others *into* jobs and not be a job *holder*.

And sadly, our school systems teach us to become great employees and not great employers.

My mentor taught me that when you believe that a job is the only way to earn money, you become trapped in the 9-to-5 cycle.

Yes, a job can earn money. But does a job earn you freedom?

I would argue no, a job does not give you freedom because you have to follow the rules of your employer.

To get your freedom, all you need is a mindset shift. That's it.

The second you realize that anyone – yes, anyone – can become a millionaire, you set yourself free of the societal cuffs.

Lesson 2: A business builds a lasting income stream

You know how many people say that "cash is king"?

Well, my mentor taught me otherwise.

Here's what I learned: Cash is good, but *cash flow* is better.

Think about it: One thing that 2020, 2021, and 2022 have taught us is that inflation can literally eat away at your cash's purchasing power. Your $100 bill could have bought you a lot more in 2020 than in 2023, for example. In fact, to give you exact numbers, $100 in 2020 would be worth $82.49 in 2023. That means your $100 lost over $17 in just 3 years. Ouch.

And that's why keeping a bunch of cash on hand is *not* always the best strategy.

You lose your purchasing power, as the last few years have illustrated.

So why cash flow?

Cash flow is the steady income stream that you would generate through a variety of ways, such as:

- Royalties.
- Capital gains.
- Rental income.
- Interest income.

- Dividend income.
- Side-hustle income.
- Building a business.

Cash flow is a steady income stream that helps supplement your lifestyle.

And what is one of the *best* ways that you can build cash flow? By building your own business.

There are many ways you can build your own business:
- You can make money on social media.
- You can become an affiliate marketing pro.
- You can build your own drop-shipping business.
- You can become a landlord and rent out real estate.
- You can build your own brick-and-mortar business.

You get the point.

So there is no one-answer-fits-all type of scenario. Every person is different, and so some people might match better with a cash flow stream that's generated from rental income while others may prefer a cash flow stream that's generated from dividend income.

You know yourself best, which means you should tailor your business to yourself.

Building a business is equal to building a lasting income stream.

Once you have built a lasting (and passive) income stream, you can retire and still live the lifestyle you want on the same income stream, pre-retirement.

Why they don't teach you this life lesson in school, I don't know.

Before we jump to the next lesson, however, I do want to point out that building a passive income stream is not very easy. It does take a lot of work up front and you probably won't see too much success initially.

In fact, you may even be in the negative (so you're spending more than you're earning) for the first few years. Times will be tough, don't forget about that.

But as you pivot, as you learn from your failures, and as you stay consistent with your business, you will likely see progress and develop a passive income stream that will help pay your bills well into retirement.

In fact, one of my favorite clients did just that: He and his wife of 40+ years now worked together to build a plastic molding manufacturing company.

The next time you go to a fast food restaurant and they give you a plastic straw or a plastic fork, spoon, and knife, for example, those utensils may have been manufactured by my client's company.

Now, my client and his wife spent *years* building up their business. They once told me they both worked into the very early morning hours, maybe 4 a.m. or 5 a.m., building up their business. He even slept on a little cot next to his machines while he was figuring out the business operations in the early years. Things were hard, they didn't get enough sleep and they were in a lot of debt because buying the machinery to produce the plastic molds was not cheap.

Even worse, most banks wouldn't even extend a loan to them because they were so young (in their late twenties) and were in the very early stages of building up their business empire. They had no track record and so the banks refused to give them loans. To secure funding to buy the machines to produce the plastic molds, my client and his wife had to go to alternative lenders who charged *massive* interest rates – almost double that of what the bank would have charged them.

It was not an easy time, and over the next 10 years or so, they were fighting to simply put a loaf of bread on the kitchen table and keep the lights on. But, with time, they sorted out their business. They started specializing in a hyper niche. They understood their clientele better. And so, the profits started slowly rolling in.

Now, about 30 years later, my client and his wife are in their seventies and are still continuing with their business – but are not involved in the business on a day-to-day basis. In fact, their manufacturing business now virtually runs on auto pilot, molding the plastic literally 24/7. They have only a handful of minimum wage employees working for them to package the plastic utensils and ship them off to the respective companies.

Now *that's* a great example of how building a passive income stream can be accomplished and help you live the life you want and deserve well into retirement.

Was it an easy success?

Absolutely not.

It was difficult, it was perilous, and it took almost a decade before my client and his wife saw some sort of light at the end of the proverbial tunnel. But they kept at it, which, ultimately, separated them from the competition.

Now, they are traveling the world and printing money in their sleep.

Lesson 3: Don't trade your freedom for money

As an employee, you trade your time and freedom for money.

And most often, working for someone else means you're working to build their dreams and not *your* dreams.

In fact, a whopping 85% of employees are unhappy with their jobs.[3]

That's a staggering number of people.

Imagine going to work every day, for 40 hours (or more) per week, working in a job you dread (just like my mentor did in the beginning), for people you don't like, spending time away from your family and loved ones.

That's no way to go through life.

Are you unhappy with your job?

If you even have just a remote glimmer of doubt, then you know where you stand.

And that's OK.

Because you can change your trajectory – no matter how old or how young you are.

My mentor taught me that as an employee, you work long hours, you are stressed, and you are always on the clock.

But, assuming you're building a business you love and are passionate about, your work won't feel like a chore. Instead, it will feel like freedom – or like you are building your path toward freedom.

So, if you choose a job you love (and are somewhat proficient in the field), and pour your time and energy into your work, then you'll likely have a much higher chance of becoming successful versus if you were unhappy and only worked the necessary hours for your paycheck.

I'll share another story of a friend of mine. He was the former vice president of a world-renowned finance and investment company, managing over $2 trillion.

I remember talking to him a while back, asking him about his number one lesson that he learned in his life.

His reply?

"Love the job you do."

I asked him to expand a little more on that statement, and he explained that if you are employed in a company, you will probably have to stay late some days or go into more detail on certain projects or come up with creative solutions. And if you don't enjoy that job or role, chances are your creativity and your eagerness to go above and beyond will be limited. Staying an extra 10 minutes late will probably feel like agony for you.

On the contrary, if you're in a job that you love, then staying 20 or even 40 minutes late probably won't bother you because you already enjoy doing the work you do. You enjoy talking about your job's subject with your employees. It lights a fire in your heart. And it's very hard to fake that fire.

While I'm not saying that you should jump ship immediately from your current job if you're not the biggest fan, I do think it's important to start thinking about alternatives.

I think it's important to think about what *you* want out of this life and start tailoring your path to your needs.

Maybe that means you'll start a side hustle that you really enjoy (like gardening or photography), which won't feel like a job to you and yet you still make a little extra income. Or maybe that means you start polishing your resume and send it to some job openings in the industry or sector in which you would like to work. It could mean a bunch of things.

My best advice though here would be to take things slow, methodically, and systematically. There is no need to quit your job right now.

But now should be the time where you start putting a plan in place if you are unhappy in your current position. That's exactly what I did when I left my six-figure corporate job. In fact, I had started putting the plan and the pieces in place about three years before I left my job.

As you may know, I'm a very conservative person when it comes to money management. I don't like jumping into any unnecessary risks because I like taking calculated risk. That's just my nature.

So I carefully planned every step of the way by connecting with people who already had taken the jump from full-time work to now running their own business to doing online research and more. By understanding what lay ahead of my journey, I felt a lot more comfortable when I finally typed up my resignation letter. I knew *exactly* what I was getting myself into. I had a plan in place and was ready to execute it.

Lesson 4: As an employee, your income potential is limited by your employer

I've already mentioned this lesson in the past, but I think it's so important that it deserves its own spot in this list.

As an employee, your income is directly tied to the amount of time you give to your employer and the details in your work contract. Sometimes, even, your income may be tied to how well you know your employer, especially if you're working in a smaller business.

Let me share a quick story with you.

One of my best friends, let's call her Jane, started working in the wealth management world by joining a small, boutique firm first. Jane was the firm's very first intern. Jane was also the very first person who did not personally know the founder of the firm. Every other employee before her knew, somehow, the founder of the firm previously.

That was tough.

In fact, Jane later shared with me that virtually every firm associate knew how to play golf (minus her) and connect with the boss of the firm (who also liked golf) outside of office hours. The closer these associates were with the boss, the more incentives, clients, raises, promotions, and so on they were given.

Jane soon realized that her office environment would not give her the growth runway that she needed in order to build the career she wanted. Because she didn't play golf with her CEO, Jane felt like the CEO would not give her as many opportunities as the other associates. And so she left.

Of course, Jane's example is probably more on the extreme side – but let me tell you, these scenarios can and do happen if you are an employee. Your salary and your opportunities are directly tied to your boss or CEO.

My mentor also reminded me that as an employee, your creative mind is often suppressed.

Why?

Because we are told to do a job in a certain way. We are given guidelines and rules. Many times, employees are not given the creative liberty to express themselves in their own, unique way. The employees must stick within the guidelines.

Unless you work for innovative companies like Google, Apple, new age digital firms, or other start-ups for example, you probably won't be encouraged to think "outside of the box."

The salary we earn from our 9 to 5 is the price we pay in exchange for building someone else's future – and not ours.

Realizing that I was building someone else's dream and not mine was pretty gut-wrenching when I was working in corporate America.

I soon realized that I was leaving so much of my own potential on the table. For example, there were many times where I had suggested changing our conventional approach to working with clients. But because my suggestions were not in line with the "status quo" of the firm, my ideas were immediately shot down by upper management.

At first, I thought that upper management was right. I thought that my ideas were bad. But after some time to myself, I realized that my ideas were actually really good – and could have made the company a lot of money in the long run.

This experience also showed me that it was time to shift gears and open a new chapter in my life: Running my own business. It was time for me to believe in myself and in my ability to succeed as a business owner, which is when I started my financial platform, The Millennial Money Woman.

If you are a business owner and an entrepreneur, there is no income limit.

When I started my platform, I didn't think I would be writing this book, or building a course, or speaking at international financial workshop events, or let alone running an international personal finance community, teaching people all over the world how to build the life they want.

Never would I have thought that when I first started my business venture.

But all of that did happen. And that's because I had creative control over my business. Whether my business succeeded or failed was entirely up to me. And while that feeling is absolutely scary and daunting, it was also exhilarating and freeing. I could literally pivot the business any way I wanted to – because I own it, and can decide its direction.

Of course, being a business owner also means more risk – but that also means more potential reward.

The very first $11 that I earned from my business felt like I had just won the lottery.

Earning your first dollar from your own business just hits differently.

I had quite literally earned $100,000s from my salaried job, so earning $11 from my own business should not have excited me. I normally would not have even raised an eyebrow at making $11.

But boy, was I thrilled.

In fact, I even remember the *day* where I made my first $11. It was a cold November morning. I had just rolled out of bed and had swiped through the latest notifications on my phone. And there was an email notification, with the subject headline saying, "You made money."

I rubbed the sleep out of my eyes when I saw that headline, thinking it was a scam or a wrong email . . . but alas, I actually made money. It was the sweetest $11 of my life. When I clicked on the actual email, which confirmed the amount I had made (while sleeping, no less!), I jumped up and probably ran through the house screaming!

My little dog probably had no idea what was going on at the time, but he gleefully ran with me, nipping at my heels while I was parading around my phone with the email opened on its screen.

In fact, earning my first $11 from my own business shattered a glass ceiling: The second I knew I could earn money from running my own platform, I realized I could do *anything* with my business.

And that was *exactly* the confidence I needed to build a business empire.

Now that you know the four incredibly important lessons I learned from my millionaire mentor, let me share four tips with you that I learned while building my own six-figure business over the past three years.

Let's jump right in.

Building a Business

Before I move into the next chapter, I wanted to take some time to share some tips if you are thinking about building your own business and joining the entrepreneurial club.

Tip 1: Do your research

Have you ever thought or dreamed about starting your own business?

Maybe you've done some preliminary research, dreamed about where you would open your business or how many employees you would hire.

If that's you, then you're already one step further than most people.

You're already *thinking* like an entrepreneur.

But, before you dive head-first to build your enterprise, do your research.

The worst thing you can do is to quit your job on the spot and start your business from scratch – without any market research.

Why am I saying this?

I'm warning you about this because I know someone firsthand who made this very fatal mistake.

He was a young professional, probably 28 or 29 at the time, earning about $130,000 per year. He was very smart and had a very bright future ahead of him.

Let's call this young professional Geoff. Geoff worked in corporate America, also in finance. He was a great salesman and had befriended all of the "important" partners in his firm. They loved him and from my conversations with Geoff, the partners were ready to give him a substantial promotion that would propel Geoff into a top 2% earning position at the ripe age of 30.

Things were going great for him.

However, like so many people, 85% to be exact, Geoff absolutely hated his job. He didn't like his clients. He didn't like his industry. He didn't like the partners in his firm.

One day (before I first met Geoff), this young man decided that he wanted to pivot. He wanted to start a new business in a niche he wasn't familiar with (public relations).

Now that is a pretty big shift – moving from finance to public relations, wouldn't you say?

Now, Geoff is a smart guy. He graduated at the top of a prestigious university, he came from virtually no money, and he had built up a pretty solid nest egg for being in his late twenties. Again, things were looking really good for him.

But, unfortunately, Geoff jumped the gun. He didn't do his research. He didn't even talk to anyone who was already in the public relations industry. Nope. Instead, Geoff simply up and quit his job, diving head-first into his new business venture.

Yes, Geoff was an entrepreneur, but he made a silly mistake. He didn't do his research.

And that's why he literally burned through *all* of his savings (which were around $150,000) in just six months, his fiancée left him, he lost his two homes, and he ultimately lost his business.

Why?

He didn't commit the time and market research before opening his business.

He quit his job first and *then* opened his business, learning by doing.

That's an example of how *not* to start your entrepreneurial journey.

I think that a lot of people learn better through hands-on activities, but if we're talking about your livelihood – your paycheck – that's another story. You should be taking *calculated* risks – not *unnecessary* risks like Geoff.

Remember back to when I shared a little bit about my journey transitioning from my 9-to-5 job to my full-time business? I took *years* carefully planning every detail of my switch.

If you're thinking about building a business, then maybe take an approach that's in between mine and Geoff's.

Here are the exact steps of what I would have done if I were Geoff:

- I would have continued working at my full-time job while doing market research on the side.
- In fact, I would stop going above and beyond on my full-time job. I would be in "maintenance mode," while researching my business opportunity.
- I would reach out to people in my network like professors, colleagues, friends, or even friends of friends in that particular industry, and ask them to grab lunch with me so I could pick their brains about their experience in public relations
- If I believed that the business idea and the industry would be profitable – and that I would actually enjoy the work – only then would I have started laying the foundation by building my business on the side. I would do all of this *while* continuing to work my full-time job

- I would dedicate about two hours each week day (Monday through Friday) and at least five hours each weekend to my business for at least the first year (consistency is key).
- Once I start earning enough money per month to support my basic living expenses, *only then* would I have considered quitting my full-time job and dedicating 100% of my time to my new business.
- *Before* I quit my full-time job, I would have also ensured that I have enough cash on the sidelines (about three to six months' worth of basic living expenses) just in case I need the money.

If you're wondering what happened to Geoff, here's the rest of the story:

He sadly quit his business about a year into it (even though he was starting to see some income). And honestly, I think his business had massive potential – his idea certainly could have disrupted the current industry – but he just didn't give it enough time. He didn't give it enough time because he ran out of cash and couldn't find any investors.

Why did he run out of cash?

Because instead of building the business on the side while continuing to work his full-time, six-figure job (and saving more money), he hurried into his business venture. Geoff basically wasted six precious months in just research that he could have otherwise done while still working his full-time job and earning a steady paycheck.

After quitting his business, Geoff moved back with his parents and took up a new job in . . . can you guess? That's right: His old industry, finance. Did Geoff have his happy ending? Not yet, sadly.

I truly think that the number one reason why Geoff failed at his business was not because of his idea or work ethic or anything like that. I think it was because he just didn't do his research.

So, if you're thinking about building a business, then I've listed some suggestions below to help you on your journey:

- **Interview potential customers to figure out their pain points and how your business could potentially solve their problems.** [Remember, when you provide a solution, money will follow.]

- **Shadow industry experts to get a feel for "a day in their life." Figure out if this is a business you actually want to get involved in.** [You'd be surprised at how many people are happy to help you.]
- **Ask someone from your local community, or even a mentor of yours, to become your business advisor – or to join your "advisory board."** [It's always good to have different, helpful perspectives as you build a business, and most advisory board members would do this pro bono – or for free.]
- **Research your country and/or state laws to ensure your business complies with them.** [You may have to file for business licenses or permits in order to even operate your company in the state you are in.]
- **Consider titling your business as an LLC or other type of business entity.** [Renaming your business as an LLC or other business entity, like an S-Corporation, may help with anonymity, taxes, creditors, etc.]
- **Determine if you need to secure financing to help pay for your company start-up costs.** [You may want to research in advance whether you need to secure bank loans, loans from family or friends (which I don't recommend), loans from the Small Business Administration (SBA), etc.]
- **Research your competitors.** [Figure out why your potential competitors are so popular. What are they doing that you could refine and improve? What are they doing that turns customers off?]
- **Research barriers to entry.** [Determine what barriers to entry you may face. Is your industry saturated? Does it cost a lot of money to open a business in your industry? And so on.]
- **Research the risks involved.** [What are the risks involved in this business? Could it be your livelihood? Could it be your family's livelihood? Are you willing to risk and potentially lose everything?]

Remember that to open a business, you don't need a college degree.

You don't even need a high school degree (although I would encourage you to at minimum complete your high school diploma).

In fact, some of the wealthiest people in the world dropped out of high school (like Sir Richard Branson, founder of Virgin Group) or college (Steve Jobs, founder of Apple) to start their multimillion- or multibillion-dollar companies.

I'm not saying that you're guaranteed to build a billion-dollar business, but I am saying that nothing should hold you back from trying. Not even your current situation.

In fact, there is SO much free information out there. For example, you can access free guides on YouTube, on social media platforms like X or on websites like *Forbes*, *Entrepreneur*, Bloomberg, Kiplinger, and so on. You can even buy courses from experienced industry experts on platforms like Udemy or Coursera. These two platforms also offer access to online classes from top universities like MIT, Yale, Harvard, and so on.

Case in point: You don't need to spend $100,000s on a business degree to start a business. Instead, utilize the resources around you.

Tip 2: Create a business plan

The next step is to build your business plan.

A business plan is essentially the framework (or foundation) of how you will run your business. It outlines a lot of the things you will need to start building your business, like a business budget and a breakdown of the expenses.

The important thing to remember about business plans, however, is that they are often merely hypothetical or theoretical. As we know, life often has many different plans for us, so while we sit and carefully plan out our future business, chances are, the business plan won't be carried out exactly as it is on paper. That's completely OK.

In fact, I learned a very important lesson from my mentor about business plans. He said that your business plan is a work in progress. According to my mentor, the second the plan hits the printer, it's already outdated because things just change so fast in business.

If you want to survive as a business owner, you must adapt to the changing times.

And as the cliché saying goes, "The only constant in life is change."

Especially in this technology-driven age, you have to stay current or else your business will no longer be relevant to your stakeholders.

That could mean:

- Use more social media.
- Adapt to new digital technologies.
- Adapt your communication style with your audience.

Here are a few additional things to consider as you start building your business plan:
- Determine your budget.
- Determine your branding.
- Determine if you need a website.
- Determine your financial projections.
- Determine your product's or service's price point.
- Determine how you plan to engage with your audience.

When I created my first business plan, I probably took 30 hours or more to write it and refine it. It probably also took me such a long time because I had literally no idea what I was doing!

To find some sort of guidance, I must have stayed up several nights, Googling the keyword phrase "how to write a business plan." I kid you not. I scoured hundreds of free resources to get a better idea of *what* it was that I needed to incorporate into a good business plan. While Google did help me out to some extent, I called up my mentor and asked him for help after going in what seemed like an endless circle.

My mentor had drafted multiple business plans in the past, so he had some good suggestions on how to optimize my time and energy when building a business plan. My business plan was *nothing* fancy. But it did help me start thinking bigger picture. And it set the foundation for my future platform.

Taking from this experience, I would say that my biggest tip is (assuming you aren't an expert in creating business plans) to ask your mentors or other industry leaders for advice when drafting your business plan.

Don't be afraid to ask for help.

If you don't ask, you don't get.

And what's the worst thing that can happen? They say "no"? OK, if that's the case, ask someone else until you get a "yes"!

Because I had already established a very solid and long-term professional relationship with my mentor, I knew I could rely on him for insight and help. So, I asked my mentor to review my business plan with me. We met up in a Starbucks (if you remember, my mentor *loves* tea, coffee, and croissants). I bought the first round of coffee for us, while I showed him my progress so far. He took about 45 minutes out of his day to give me tips and advice on how I could make a killer business plan.

I know not everyone has a mentor in their network with extensive knowledge on creating business plans. And that's perfectly OK.

If you fall in that category, then you may want to check out some professional online courses that walk you through creating a business plan. Or, you may want to network so you *can* find that person with start-up experience – and that's exactly my next tip.

Tip 3: Network

Assuming you've built your business plan and researched your niche market, it's time to start networking.

In fact, whenever you have the chance, you probably want to start networking.

My mentor taught me that my network is my net worth.

You can have degrees from the fanciest Ivy League schools in the world, but that doesn't guarantee that you'll get the best job.

In fact, my mentor taught me that the No. 1 predictor of your success is the breadth and depth of your network.

So what does this mean for you?

To build a successful business you should
- Build your network online.
- Build your network offline.
- Become involved in your local community.
- Provide thoughtful and genuine value to your audience.
- Become known as a thought leader within your community.

The best way to build a genuine network is to give first and receive later.
Think about it:

> If someone randomly reaches out to you via email and asks you for advice, are you going to give them your time and your advice – that likely took you months, if not years, to learn – for free?

The answer is probably "no."

Now, think about this scenario: One of your audience members has consistently engaged with you over the past few weeks or months, offering a lot of value. You can see they are genuinely interested in you, your mission, and your work.

This same person then reaches out to you one day, asking for your advice.

Would you be more likely to give them your time, knowing they gave you something first?

The answer is probably "yes."

And that's how you should approach your networking and relationship building: give first, ask later.

While I'm by no means the best networker, I would say that I have met some pretty incredible people from all over the world, so I want to make sure I share some of my networking strategies with you.

First, I actually wouldn't even call it "networking." Why? Because I feel like we all cringe when we hear the word "network." It sounds forced, phony, and fake. Ugh. I shiver just thinking about networking.

So instead, I try to reframe the activity from "networking" to "befriending." Finding friends, or befriending people sounds *so* much better than networking, right?

And think about it: You are probably *much* more likely to do business with a *friend* than with someone you don't like or barely know, right?

That's exactly the nature of the business world. You are much more likely to conduct business with friends or people you trust. So, instead of networking, consider that you are simply at the event to make friends. Get to know the other person. Ask them questions about themselves. Get their business card and then ask to meet them for lunch or coffee/tea at some point in the future.

In fact, I would say that grabbing a one-on-one lunch with people you meet at networking events is probably one of the best and fastest ways to create business connections. It's that one-on-one time that really counts.

And the best part?

You don't even have to meet for lunch that many times. Remember that what counts is the quality of time that you spend with them and not the *quantity* of time that you spend with them.

Quality over quantity always.

The second piece of advice I would give you before entering any networking or "befriending" event is to set a goal for yourself. It can be any type of goal, but go into the event with a goal.

So, for example, every time I met with my young professional group, my goal was to meet at least one new person at each event. That's it.

My goal was low pressure.

Why did it work out for me?

Because I tried to focus on quality time. I wanted to connect with someone new and genuinely get to know them. This strategy worked – at least it did for me.

Tip 4: Don't quit your job until you're ready

The last tip for building your business is actually committing to your business.

On paper, this sounds easy.

In real life, this is a task that's much, much harder to do.

Think about it:

- You'll be leaving your stable paycheck.
- You'll be leaving the safety of your job.
- You'll be leaving a steady work schedule.
- You'll be leaving your employee mentality.
- You'll be leaving your presumably cheap healthcare (if you live the United States).

. . . And you're exchanging all of that safety, security, and stability for the unknown.

That's pretty scary.

And that's why entrepreneurs are typically bold people.

But it's important to understand that entrepreneurs (at least most of them) take calculated risks.

In other words, they do their research, they take time to think about their business plan, and they build their network *before* they actually quit their 9-to-5 job and dedicate themselves to their start-up business.

Let me tell you that when I made the switch from my 9-to-5 job to my full-time business venture, I was pretty nervous. While I had done the research and I had everything planned out, I still didn't like the feeling of not knowing whether I would actually earn enough in any given month to cover my expenses.

I had no idea.

There were so many times where I worked 15+ hour days, trying to improve my business . . . but it just *never* seemed like I made any progress. I was grumpy a lot of the time because I didn't see progress. I was frustrated. Upset. And I was scared.

I was scared that I made the wrong choice – leaving my cushy six-figure job to build a business that wasn't exactly making as much money as I had originally projected. That's right; I honestly thought that I would be "printing" cash the second I left my full-time job. So wrong.

While I did make some money – between $1,000 and $5,000 per month – it was *barely* enough money to cover my living expenses. Barely.

And I was working much harder with so much more uncertainty than what I was used to at my 9-to-5 job. Welcome to the world of entrepreneurship.

Instead of being dependent on my boss for a paycheck, I was now dependent on Google, on the X algorithm (that has changed *massively* since Elon Musk took over the platform), and I was dependent on the latest trends in finance.

So, while, yes, you're no longer dependent on your boss for a paycheck, you are now dependent on many other factors that can still determine how much money you earn.

I think a lot of people don't realize how scary it can be, going into business by yourself. Your success is completely based on your own effort. And sometimes *that's* not even enough, like when Google or other platforms randomly change their algorithm on you and you need to adapt ASAP – or you might not be able to adapt.

There are so many people that come up to me and say, "Fiona, if there are so many online influencers that make $30,000 or more per month online, then why am I not making that money?"

Truth be told, these influencers are the exception.

There are *so* many others out there who are trying, too. And they may succeed – absolutely. But the reason why I am sharing this with you now is to teach you to lower your expectations initially.

Don't go into your business thinking that you're going to be earning five-figures in your first month. Maybe you will. But it's unlikely.

And the worst thing I see is that people really *do* think they'll earn that much money in their first few months . . . only to lose motivation and then give up completely.

Just . . . try to stay realistic with your income expectations.

So here is my advice if you are thinking about opening your own business but are still working in a steady 9-to-5 job.

First, take your time to build up your side hustle *while* you are still working your full-time job.

Second, push yourself to make mistakes (and fail fast) *while* you are still earning your full-time paycheck. Learn about your business and industry as much as you can *before* you actually jump head-first into the business.

Third, once your income from your start-up business somewhat matches the income from your full-time job, or at least covers your basic living expenses (like rent, groceries, medical care, etc.), only *then* consider pulling the trigger and leaving your full-time job.

The last thing you want to do is to end up like Geoff, who I mentioned in Tip 1 – who just quit his $130,000 annual salary job at 28 to start a new business from scratch (one he didn't research beforehand), just to fail and burn through his savings . . . and end up in the *same* industry he initially wanted to leave.

Not a good start.

So, here are some final tips I want to leave you with as you embark on your business journey:

- **Always track your progress.** [If you cannot measure your progress, whether good or bad, then you won't be given the chance to improve.]
- **Adjust your business plan.** [It's OK and sometimes necessary to pivot your business to adjust. Adapt or die. Think about how Amazon first started as an online bookseller. Now you can buy anything on Amazon from e-books to custom dog socks.]
- **Never stop researching.** [It's not possible to know everything. Learn every day because you never know what useful bit of information can help propel your business to the next level.]
- **Be patient.** [Remember that to have overnight success, it will take years. If you want to build a steady cash flow, you're probably going to have to work hard for a long period of time (while earning very little or nothing). Don't be discouraged if you don't see immediate success. Focus on the long-run.]
- **Be consistent.** [To achieve success, you have to be consistent with your efforts. Even if you don't see success right away, keep putting in the work and remember to track your progress. Figure out what works and adjust accordingly.]
- **Put in the effort.** [To do stellar work, you're going to have to put in the effort. Remember the statistic that I mentioned earlier – that only 3% of millionaires received an inheritance

of $1 million or more. The rest of the millionaires earned their wealth the traditional way: hard work. You're probably going to have to do the same.]

- **Be realistic.** [Have realistic expectations before you jump into your business. In fact, the best strategy here is to under promise and over deliver.]

Challenge #10: Think about a Potential Business Idea and Start Researching It

For this challenge, take some time to think about your current position at your job. Think about whether you're happy or unhappy, and think about what you are truly passionate about.

Would you feel relieved starting your own business/side hustle?

And, oftentimes, building a small side hustle could eventually transform into a well-oiled business in the future. So, perhaps you may want to start small and slowly work your way to bigger endeavors later on.

Think about your pace and your goals.

Now it's time to put your thoughts on paper and create a framework for your business plan.

Here's how:

1. Determine if you're happy in your job.
2. Determine what you would change about your job.
3. Determine if you would be comfortable starting your own business.
4. If "yes," start researching the industry that you would be most passionate about.

(Continued)

5. Research your competitors, your barriers to entry, conduct a business or industry SWOT analysis (strengths, weakness, opportunities, threads), and so on.
6. Begin connecting with like-minded entrepreneurs or people who are successful in your chosen niche. Invite them out for coffee or tea and ask if you can pick their brain with questions to get a better idea of what you could be getting yourself into.
7. Most importantly, start developing a business plan to get the fundamental business building blocks into place.

Remember this

Anyone can open a business – you do not need a fancy college degree to become an entrepreneur. Even high school dropouts managed to build multimillion and multibillion dollar companies. If they can do it, so can you.

It takes grit, passion, consistency, and hard work to succeed. And, yes, it may also take a little bit of luck.

But betting *all* of your business success on luck is not a good strategy.

If you don't take your eye off the target, you certainly have a great chance to win.

Now, take some time to think about what you picture your life to be like in 10 to 20 years from now. If you can see yourself in the same job (and being happy), then congratulations! You are very lucky because not many people are in your shoes. If you cannot see yourself holding the same job and being happy over the long term, then it might be time to start making some changes today.

Notes

1. Kolmar, Chris. (17 Nov. 2022). Entrepreneur statistics: The latest demographics and trends. [online]. Zippia. https://www.zippia.com/advice/entrepreneur-statistics/ (accessed 10 July 2023).

2. How many millionaires actually inherited their wealth? (2022). Ramsey Solutions. https://www.ramseysolutions.com/retirement/how-many-millionaires-actually-inherited-their-wealth (accessed 10 July 2023).

3. Unhappy employees' statistics: Are your employees secretly unhappy? (21 March 2023). Gitnux. https://blog.gitnux.com/unhappy-employees-statistics/#:~:text=85%25%20of%20individuals%20worldwide%20are%20unhappy%20in%20their%20jobs%2C%20according,and%20fulfilled%20in%20their%20roles (accessed 12 July 2023).

Chapter 12
Play the Tax Game

Have you ever heard this saying by Benjamin Franklin:

"In this world, nothing is certain except death and taxes."

And for the most part, it's true, right?

Only 14 countries in the world don't levy income taxes on its residents. So if you live in one of these 14 countries, you can skip over this chapter. But if you live in a country that *does* have income taxes, specifically the United States, then you probably want to read this chapter.

Because I'm going to teach you how to play the tax game.

In fact, of the 453 millionaires whom I helped get richer, 100% of them knew the tax game inside and out. And if they didn't know all of it on their own? They had help. They had accountants. They had CPAs. They had estate planning attorneys. And of course, they had wealth advisors (me!).

So, what am I trying to say with this?

If you really, truly want to build long-term wealth, then you better start learning the tax game.

Now, I jokingly tell my clients and the people I mentor to read about tax code and tax law if they are having trouble falling asleep . . . tax code does make remarkably great sleeping material.

But in a way, understanding and reading up on the latest tax litigation is important. And if you don't have the time or you just simply couldn't care any less about it, then hire someone. Yes, your accountant might charge a few thousand dollars, but trust me – if you have a good accountant – then they will pay for themselves at some point.

So, with that said, let's start talking about how *you* can use taxes to help you save more money and build long-term wealth.

Our first stop?

Investment accounts.

If you don't know yet, then this is your wake-up call: You can absolutely start building your wealth in investment accounts that will be 100% tax free when you retire (assuming you follow all of the rules). This type of account is called a Roth account. And we'll get into that later.

In fact, you could become a tax-free millionaire.

What do I mean by that?

I mean you could have saved and invested millions of dollars, and as long as that money is in the *correct* investment account, you will never have to pay another penny on that money.

Don't believe me?

Let me share an example of a real-life tax-free millionaire.

Let's rewind the clock back to 2010. In 2010, the co-founder of PayPal and chairman of Yelp, Max Levchin, became a tax-free millionaire using his Roth IRA. He sold 3.1 million shares of Yelp in his Roth IRA, which came out to be about a $10.1-million profit. *Tax free*. Normally, that sale could have cost him up to $3.7 million in taxes, assuming he was in the highest income tax bracket.[1]

But because Max played the tax game and used a tax-advantaged investment account (in this case, the Roth IRA), he legally avoided paying taxes. And as long as he doesn't withdraw the profit before he reaches 59.5, then he will not have to pay a penny in taxes.

And the crazy part?

Max STILL has 3.9 million MORE shares of Yelp left in his Roth IRA. . . . So he may actually have a $95-million tax-free Roth IRA.

Talk about the power of playing the tax game!

Now, I know Max Levchin's example is an extreme case – not many of us have $1 million or let alone $100 million. But if he can play the game, so can you.

Still not convinced the tax game can save you money?

Let's take another example. This time, Peter Thiel, another co-founder of PayPal.

He played the tax game so well that he turned his Roth IRA into a $5-billion tax-free investment vehicle. Let me repeat that. $5 BILLION, with a *b*. And as long as Peter Thiel waits until he turns 59.5 years old (which will be in April 2027), he can withdraw that money without ever having to pay a single penny in taxes.

Now the crazy part is that you can only contribute several thousand dollars into a Roth IRA every year ($6,500 if you're under 50, and $7,500 if you're age 50 or older as of 2023). So how did Peter Thiel and Max Levchin play the tax game and build a massive Roth IRA fund?

Here's how they did it.

They started investing early into their Roth IRAs with only a few thousand dollars. But the key difference is that they *knew* their company, PayPal, would be successful one day. So they bought their start-up's shares for a fraction of what they cost today.

The next step?

Peter and Max just waited for the value of the stocks to literally explode in price. They could sell their stocks whenever they wanted for the massive profit of $100+ million. And the profits? Well, they will *never* be subjected to taxes. That's as long as they don't touch their IRA until they reach 59.5 years old.

There are other, very savvy ways to play the tax game specifically with a Roth IRA (known as a Roth conversion or a mega backdoor Roth conversion), but we won't get into those for now. They can wait for another day and another book (so stay tuned!).

Now that you know it's 100% possible to play the tax game – and play it well – let's get into the nitty gritty.

Let's actually talk about how *you* can start taking advantage of the tax game – regardless of your income or savings level – and start building that long-term fortune today.

It all starts with tax-advantaged investment accounts.

So what exactly *are* tax-advantaged investment accounts?

They are a type of investment account, sometimes also known as a "qualified account" that could be one of two things:

- **Tax exempt** – Means you'll never owe a penny in taxes as long as you follow all rules.
- **Tax deferred** – Means you'll receive some sort of up-front tax benefit (like an up-front tax deduction), but you may have to pay taxes at some point in the future.

Now, you might be wondering if tax-advantaged investment accounts are legal. I have good news for you: They are! (At least in the United States.)

If you haven't opened a tax-advantaged investment account yet, then your task for this week's chapter is to start thinking about opening a tax-advantaged investment account.

We just talked about tax-advantaged accounts.

But what if you have an investment account that's *not* tax advantaged? What then?

Well, first of all, that's not a bad thing. At all!

Think about it: Just like with your investments, where you want to have some level of diversification, you also want to have some sort of diversification with your tax accounts.

That means you'll want to have some tax deferred, some tax exempt, and some nontax-advantaged investment accounts.

If you have an investment account that's not tax advantaged, then quite simply, you don't get any tax benefits. At all.

Some examples of nontax-advantaged investment accounts include:
- Revocable trusts.
- Savings accounts.

- Checking accounts.
- Joint investment accounts.
- Individual investment accounts.

Basically, you have to pay taxes on your contributions, investment profits, gains, withdrawals, and so on.

If Max Levchin had sold his 3.1 million shares of Yelp in his nontax-advantaged account, making him a $10.1-million profit, then he would have to pay taxes in the year he realized the profit.

Although nontax-advantaged investment accounts don't sound like the best deal – they're actually not that bad. And again, it comes down to tax diversification.

Let's take an individual investment account (a type of nontax-advantaged account) for an example.

The following are some tax features to note:
- You are taxed on your account contributions.
- You are taxed on any profits (assuming you trade and/or sell investments).
- You are *not* taxed on withdrawals, but typically to withdraw money, you have to sell all or a portion of your investments, which may trigger a taxable event.
- You can also be taxed on any dividend or interest income in the year of the income.

As you can see, you really don't get any tax breaks with accounts that aren't tax advantaged.

So why could an individual account (aka a nontax-advantaged account) be beneficial to you when you're playing the tax game?

It all comes down to tax diversification.

In other words, you don't *just* want to have:

- 100% of your money in Roth accounts.
- 100% of your money in pre-tax accounts.
- 100% of your money in nontax-advantaged accounts.

You want to diversify the tax nature of your accounts.

There is one additional key benefit to having a regular investment account that's not tax advantaged: **There are no contribution limits and no withdrawal limits.**

I say this because with IRAs (whether Roth or Traditional) as well as employer-sponsored retirement plans like a 401k or a 403b plan, there will always be annual contribution limits. Those annual contribution limits can be as low as $6,500 per year or as high as about $60,000 per year. But that's it.

Of course, for many of us, making a $60,000 annual contribution would be a luxury that we don't have, but as you start making more money, that does become a true concern.

In fact, with most tax-advantaged accounts, there are several strings attached, such as:

- The restrictions for you to make withdrawals.
- The eligibility requirements for you to contribute.
- The amount of money you can contribute per year.

So, if you haven't had the chance to open an individual account yet, you can do so in one of two ways:

- Traditional investment platforms like Vanguard, Charles Schwab, or Fidelity.
- Robo-advisor platforms like Acorns, M1 Finance, and so on.

Which type of platform you like really depends on your own investment preference and comfort level (e.g., if you're less experienced with investing, then a robo-advisor platform might be better suited for your needs).

Now that you know some common examples of nontax-advantaged investment accounts (savings, individual investment account, etc.), let's take a look at some of the common tax-advantaged investment accounts. These are the ones that can also help you get ahead in the tax game.

Common tax-advantaged investment accounts:
- 457b.
- 403b.
- SEP IRA.
- Roth IRA.
- Roth 401k.
- Roth 403b.
- Traditional IRA.
- Traditional 401k.
- Traditional 403b.

If your eyes glazed over, then I don't blame you. Sometimes I think "they" make finance complicated on purpose!

In fact, when I first started learning about money, I thought I was studying a different language with all of these abbreviations. So you're definitely not alone.

For those of you who are curious about what each of these tax advantaged accounts actually mean, let me explain them in more detail:

Tax-Advantaged Account	What It Does
457	Not all employers offer 457 plans, and typically, 457 plans are offered to state and local government employees or tax-exempt organizations (like nonprofits). 457 plans are similar to Traditional 401k plans, where you receive a tax deduction today, but will have to pay once you withdraw your money. The best part about 457 plans is that you receive a special 457 catch-up contribution, called the "last 3-year catch-up" which means - if you qualify - you could defer a portion of your salary in the three years before reaching the 457 plan's normal retirement age. The amount that you are allowed to defer during this special catch-up period depends on the 457 plan you are enrolled in.

Tax-Advantaged Account	What It Does
Roth 403b	Is like a 401k plan, just for government workers, nonprofits, teachers, religious workers, and so on. With a Roth 403b, you pay taxes on the contributions you make today and you don't have to pay taxes on any withdrawals you take during retirement.
Traditional 403b	Is like a 401k plan, just for government workers, nonprofits, teachers, religious workers, etc. With a Traditional 403b, you receive an income tax deduction today on any contributions you make, but you'll have to pay taxes on any withdrawals you make in the future.
Roth 401k	Not all employers offer Roth 401k plans, and you'll probably have to ask your employer if they offer them because the default option is often the Traditional 401k. With a Roth 401k, you pay taxes on the contribution you make and you don't have to pay taxes on any future withdrawals.
Traditional 401k	This is the most common type of tax-advantaged retirement plan offered by employers. With a Traditional 401k, you receive an income tax deduction today on any contributions you make, but you'll have to pay taxes on future withdrawals.

Tax-Advantaged Account	What It Does
Roth IRA	Almost anyone can open and contribute to a Roth IRA – unless you don't have earned income or you earn too much (each year, an income threshold is given). With a Roth IRA, you pay taxes on the contribution you make today and you don't have to pay taxes on any future withdrawals.
Traditional IRA	Almost anyone can open a Traditional IRA as long as you have earned income. How much (if any) of a tax deduction you receive will depend on how much you earn. With a Traditional IRA, you may receive an income tax deduction today on contributions you make, but you'll have to pay taxes on future withdrawals.
SEP IRA	SEP IRAs are common for business owners (typically single employee businesses) who want to open a tax-advantaged retirement account that's simple and cheap to process. There is no Roth SEP IRA option, so all of your money contributed will be pre-tax.

It's important to note that some employer-sponsored tax-advantaged investment accounts like a 401k or 403b plan don't actually give you the freedom to invest in whatever stocks, bonds, or other funds you want. In fact, when you enroll in your employer-sponsored retirement plan, you are given an option of typically 20 to 50 investments. That's it.

However you choose to play the tax game – whether that's by using an individual investment account or a tax advantaged investment account – the trick is to invest consistently and for the long term.

Challenge #11: Open a Tax-Advantaged Investment Account

For this week's challenge, think about the types of investment accounts you currently have.

Maybe you have one. Or maybe you don't have any open right now – which is perfectly OK too.

If you have several investment accounts, think about their tax nature. Are they "diversified" in the sense of their tax nature? Or do you have 100% of your money tied up in Roth money? Or traditional (or pre-tax) money? Or nontax-advantaged money?

Whatever your situation, *now* is the time to open an investment account and start contributing (and investing) money.

Here's what you can do next:

1. Consider opening a tax-advantaged investment account (like a Traditional IRA).
2. Consider opening a Roth IRA (assuming you are eligible).
3. Consider investing a consistent (such as a bi-weekly) amount.
4. Consider opening an individual (nontax-advantaged) account (assuming you haven't already).

How much you should contribute really depends on your own personal financial situation.

And where you should contribute first also depends on a variety of factors . . . but for most young people, you probably want to think about contributing first to a Roth IRA over a Traditional IRA.

Why?

That's *exactly* what I'm going to discuss in the next chapter!

Note

1. Jacobs, D.L. (20 March 2012). How a serial entrepreneur built a $950 million tax free Roth IRA. [online]. *Forbes.* Available at: https://www .forbes.com/sites/deborahljacobs/2012/03/20/how-facebook-billionaires-dodge-mega-millions-in-taxes/?sh=32e184e658f3 (accessed 15 July 2023).

Chapter 13

Roth IRA versus Traditional IRA

You can make a lot of moolah if you play the tax game correctly.

And I shared some examples in the previous chapter about saving *millions* of dollars – literally – if you play your cards right.

So let's jump into the two most common types of tax-advantaged investment accounts out there: The Roth IRA and the Traditional IRA.

Many people I speak to think that a Roth IRA and a Traditional IRA are actual investments. Like actual investment funds or exchange-traded funds (ETFs). But that's not the case here. A Roth IRA is just a *type* of account. A Traditional IRA is just a *type* of account.

Both Roth IRAs and Traditional IRAs offer very similar – if not the same – types of investment options. That could be literally *thousands* of investment options. And you can absolutely invest your money into these options using either account.

The difference?

How your profits, withdrawals, and dividends or interest income are treated.

Let's start this chapter out with a quick example:

Let's say that I'm a 65 year old retiree. And let's say that I had saved and invested a total balance of $1 million in my Traditional IRA account.

Now, let's say I want to withdraw that $1 million.
How much money do I actually have left?
Many of you might be scratching your heads, thinking that I'm asking you a trick question . . . but that's not the case (sadly). I actually *don't* have $1 million dollars in my retirement account. In fact, I have much less than $1 million.
Why?
Because the *second* I withdraw any of that money from my account, that money is taxable. All of it. So in reality, depending on my income tax bracket and several other factors, I probably only have around $700,000 in actual money that I can use for retirement.
Yikes. That's about $300,000 all going to taxes. And *that* is the downfall of the Traditional IRA.
Now let's look at the same example again. But, instead of using a Traditional IRA, let's use a Roth IRA (and this goes back to the previous chapter's example with Max Levchin and Peter Thiel, the co-founders of PayPal).
If I had a total balance of $1 million in my Roth IRA account, then how much money would I actually have? I would actually have $1 million. It's ALL mine!
I am going to warn you here . . . this section might get a bit dry, but try to stick with me (no pun intended!).
First, let's talk about *who* should be opening a Roth IRA. Because Roth IRAs are actually not for everyone. In fact, the government even went so far as to put income limits on Roth IRA eligibility.
That means if you make over a certain amount of money each year (e.g., if you are a single tax filer as of 2023 and earn more than $153,000), then you will be disqualified from contributing to the Roth IRA!

As always, there are exceptions and there are most certainly tax loopholes where even someone making $10 million could be making Roth contributions (but we'll get into that another time).

For right now, just note that Roth IRAs are typically a great investment account for new investors and for those who are just starting out in their careers. That's because when you are just starting out in your career, you are probably at the lower stages of your income earning potential, so paying taxes on your Roth IRA contributions probably won't be too big of a hit for you. I'll explain more later, so stay tuned.

Now, before I go into any more detail, let's talk about some of the technical differences between a Roth IRA and a Traditional IRA.

Roth Account	Traditional Account
No tax deduction in the year of contribution	Tax deduction in the year of contribution
No tax on profits – as long as you don't withdraw money	No tax on profits – as long as you don't withdraw money
Withdrawals are tax-free (as long as you follow certain Roth account rules)	Withdrawals are taxed as ordinary income

If you're in a higher tax bracket, you'll likely want to consider accounts like the Traditional IRA or Traditional 401k since your contributions will be deducted immediately from your income tax returns.

If your contributions will be deducted, then:

- Your tax bill will be lower for this year.
- But you'll have to pay taxes once you withdraw from your Traditional IRA.

You're basically gambling on current versus future income tax brackets. That's really what it is.

I've created a quick guide to help you better decide when a Roth or a Traditional IRA might be best for your situation:

	Consider Contributing to a Roth Account	Consider Contributing to a Traditional Account

• You are young
  • You have relatively low income
  • You expect your income to increase
	Yes	No

• You are close to retirement
  • You have a relatively high income
  • You expect your income to stay the same during retirement
	No	Yes

Typically speaking, a Roth account is often the more preferred choice for young investors who are just starting out in their career.

Below are some reasons why you may want to consider opening a Roth account over a Traditional account:
- If you're starting out in a new career, you're probably in a lower tax bracket now than what you'll be during retirement, so it might make sense to pay taxes on contributions today and not pay taxes on withdrawals during retirement (assuming you withdraw after 59.5 years old).
- If you're young, you can take advantage of the long-term (and tax-free) growth achieved through compounding interest if you invest in a Roth account (remember, with Traditional accounts, you'll have to pay taxes on anything you withdraw).
- Simply put, what you have in a Roth account is truly 100% your money (think back to our previous example). On the contrary,

in a Traditional account, your account value really isn't what you get to live on – because you'll have to subtract out a percentage for taxes.

By "Traditional account," I mean a Traditional IRA or a Traditional 401k – where you'll have a tax deduction in the year of the contribution and you'll have to pay taxes when you withdraw money.

Similarly, when I say "Roth account," I mean either a Roth IRA or a Roth 401k. They are pretty much the same thing, just one is an employer-sponsored plan with higher contribution limits (the Roth 401k plan) and one is an account that virtually anyone can open who has earned income in the United States (the Roth IRA).

There is one key rule you need to remember: You cannot touch your money – in either a Roth IRA or a Traditional IRA – until you turn 59.5 years old.

If you do withdraw money before age 59.5, then you may:

- Owe income taxes on the distributions.
- Be subject to an additional 10% penalty tax on the total withdrawal amount.

The good news is that there are, as always, some exceptions to the early withdrawal rules.

The following are some examples in which you will NOT have to pay the 10% additional early distribution tax (but you may still be subject to income taxes on the withdrawals):

- Death.
- Disability.
- Domestic Relations [you get a divorce and under a QDRO, a Qualified Domestic Relations Order, you need to distribute a portion of your IRA funds to your ex-spouse].
- Education [you can pay for tuition and other "qualified" higher education expenses for yourself, your spouse, children, or grandchildren].
- Homeowner [if you are a first-time homebuyer you can withdraw up to $10,000].

Like I said before, there are some additional exceptions, but these are the main ones.

Now, if your goal is to build as much long-term wealth as possible using an IRA, then opening a tax-advantaged investment account and investing in the stock market may be your best move.

In fact, the rising stock market has created about 300,000 U.S. millionaires.[1]

The trick to build a million dollars or more in your retirement account is to invest consistently and for the long term.

So with that said, let's take a look at *which* investment accounts everyone should open and start making investment contributions in.

Step 1: First, get access to an employer-matching contribution.

If you are working for an employer and your employer offers a 401k or 403b for its employees, this is your ticket to get free money.

Ask your employer or HR department (Human Resources) if they offer an employer-sponsored retirement plan (like a 401k plan or a 403b plan). If the answer is "yes," your next question should be whether they make employer-matching contributions.

An employer-matching contribution is essentially free money.

Would you pick up a $100 bill or $1,000 just lying on the sidewalk with your name literally printed on the money?

I sure would!

Well, that's exactly what an employer-matching contribution is, as well: It's free money just waiting to be deposited in your personal retirement account.

The catch?

You have to be the first one to contribute to your employer-sponsored retirement plan. There is typically a formula that is used to calculate how much your employer matches your contributions by, but we won't get into the details.

Instead, let me share an example: Your employer would promise to contribute 100% of the first 3% of your salary.

What the heck does that mean?

Here's a real-life scenario using the preceding numbers:

- You earn $50,000 per year.
- You contribute 3% of your salary ($50,000) to your 401k plan, which is equal to $1,500.
- Because you contributed 3% of your salary to your 401k plan, now your employer matches 100% of your 3% contribution (which means your employer will also contribute $1,500).

This is literally one of the *very few* legit ways to DOUBLE your investment contributions with pretty much no risk.

Here's another real-life scenario using the same previous numbers:

- You earn $50,000 per year.
- You contribute 5% of your salary ($50,000) to your 401k plan, which is equal to $2,500.
- Your employer will only contribute up to the first 3% of your salary ($1,500), so even though you contributed $2,500, your employer will contribute only $1,500 to your 401k plan.

I personally encourage people to make a contribution that's much greater than whatever the employer match is. However, *at minimum*, make a contribution so that you get 100% of the employer match (and in this case, it would be contributing a minimum of 3% of your annual salary).

In other words, do what I'm going to share in this example (using the same previous numbers):

- You earn $50,000 per year.
- You contribute 2% of your salary ($50,000) to your 401k plan, which is equal to $1,000.
- Your employer will only contribute up to the first 3% of your salary, so even though your employer *could* make a contribution of $1,500 because you only contributed 2% of your salary (or $1,000), your employer will only match your $1,000 contribution.

In other words, you're leaving $500 on the table. Or, as in our previous example, on the sidewalk.

I don't know about you, but I would be *livid* if I left $500 of my own money on the sidewalk.

Keep in mind that this scenario is *only an example,* and each employer plan is different – so make sure you understand the jargon within the plan to know how much money you can contribute to get the employer match (if there even is one). Some companies, in fact, may not offer an employer match. Some may.

Not sure what your employer does?

Reach out to your HR department directly. If you don't have an HR department, then talk to your direct boss who can likely point you in the right direction.

Here's another tip to maximize your money with employer-sponsored plans:

> Ask your HR department (or your direct boss) if they offer Roth 401k or Roth 403b plans.

Now, not all employers offer Roth options. In fact, the Roth plans are pretty new (the Roth 401k, e.g., first went into effect on January 1, 2006). And some employers may only offer the Traditional 401k option.

However, if your employer *does* offer the Roth 401k (or Roth 403b) option, then you may want to consider opening a Roth account instead of a Traditional account.

The following are some benefits of having a Roth 401k/403b plan:

- Your money is safe from creditors.
- You can save more than in your Roth IRA.
- In most cases, your employer will give you a match.
- You don't have to pay taxes on any profit or withdrawals from the Roth money you contribute (as long as you withdraw after age 59.5).

Do any of these Roth 401k benefits sound familiar?

They should because the majority of the Roth 401k benefits will match the benefits from Roth IRAs.

Here are some potential drawbacks of having a Roth 401k/ 403b plan:

- Limited investment options (due to the nature of an employer-sponsored plan).
- Could have higher fees than IRAs (again, due to the nature of an employer-sponsored plan).
- You may have to pay taxes on withdrawals of any *employer* contributions (which are counted separately from *your* Roth contributions).

To clarify, *employer* contributions will always be taxed the same as a Traditional IRA contribution (meaning any withdrawals from employer contributions will be taxed as ordinary income). Any *employee* contributions (so whatever you contribute and invest) will *not* be taxed assuming you withdraw after 59.5 years old.

Now, as always, there may be some cases where it might not make sense to contribute to a Roth 401k or a Roth 403b account.

These cases may include the following situations:

- Your employer does not offer a matching program.
- The investment fees within your 401k or 403b account are too expensive.
- You're in a very high income tax bracket and need a tax break in the current year of your contributions (so you would use a Traditional 401k or 403b account).

Alright, we just dissected Step 1: If you are eligible to open an employer-sponsored retirement plan *and* you can get an employer matching contribution, go get it.

Let's move on to Step 2: Open a Roth IRA and make the maximum permissible annual contribution.

In fact, did you know that 25% of Millennials *already* have a Roth IRA in place?[2]

Now, keep in mind that there are pretty strict rules and limitations in place if you are trying to contribute to a Roth IRA. In fact, not everyone can contribute.

Here are the two main rules you need to know if you are eligible for a Roth IRA:

- You have earned income (e.g., from wages, tips, salary, etc.).
- You don't earn too much money.

That's right; you read the last point right.

The Roth IRA has set guidelines that prohibit people who earn too much money from contributing to a Roth IRA (now there are ways around this by using strategies like a mega backdoor Roth conversion or a Roth conversion, but we'll skip over that for now).

There is something called an income limit. If you make more than this income limit, then you are not eligible to contribute directly to a Roth IRA. Now each and every year these income limits change (typically they increase with inflation), so it's important to stay on top of these income limits.

However, for the 2023 year, if you make more than the following amount of money per year, you will *not* be able to contribute directly to a Roth IRA:

- If you are a single income tax filer, your income limit is: $153,000.
- If you are married and file your taxes jointly (MFJ), your income limit is: $228,000.

Another piece of advice regarding IRAs in general:

You need to have **earned** income.

Earned income is defined as income such as wages, tips, salary. So earned income does *not* include income like:

- Pension income.
- Annuity income.
- Most rental income.
- Social Security benefits.
- Worker's compensation benefits.

The contribution limit for the 2023 year (assuming you are under age 50) is $6,500. However, if you earned $4,000 in 2023, then the maximum amount of money you can possibly contribute to either IRA – Roth or Traditional – is $4,000.

You can never contribute *more* than your earned income number for a particular year.

If you haven't opened a Roth IRA yet, then you can do so either using:

- Traditional platforms.
- Robo-advisor platforms.

Traditional platforms include well-known broker dealers or custodians like Charles Schwab, Vanguard, or Fidelity. These platforms are have been around for years, have a good track record, are global, and hold virtually billions of dollars of assets.

But, the downside is that there is a learning curve associated with opening an investment account on one of these platforms, such as you'll have to understand the technology of the investment platform, connect your bank account with the platform so you can make contributions and withdrawals, understand where the buy/sell buttons are to place trades, and have a general understanding of the platform's charts and graphs to know how your money is allocated.

The second option is opening an IRA account using robo-advisors like Acorns, M1 Finance, and the like. These investment platforms are generally designed for more of the beginner investor; they are more colorful, and they offer more guidance and more handholding. The downside, though, is that these platforms typically *don't* have a great track record when it comes to history, they are not global, and they are not as proven as the "traditional" platforms are.

Now that we've talked about Roth IRAs, let's move on to Step 3.

Assuming you've maxed out your Roth IRA, earned 100% of your employer-matching contribution and maybe even contributed *more* money to your employer-sponsored retirement plan, *now* is the time to think about opening an individual, nontax-advantaged account.

And this is Step 3: Open an individual (or joint, if you are married) investment account.

We've already reviewed nontax-advantaged accounts and how they help diversify your tax picture. We've also talked about the tax implications of taxable investment accounts.

And finally, let's talk about Step 4.

Step 4: Open a Traditional IRA (or contribution to a Traditional 401k plan, e.g.) because you are in a higher income bracket.

If you remember earlier, when we spoke about playing the tax game, I mentioned that Traditional IRA accounts give you an up-front tax deduction.

In other words, if you contribute $6,500 to a Traditional IRA in 2023, then you also get a tax deduction in 2023 for that $6,500 contribution. However, when you take your money out of the Traditional IRA (remember, after age 59.5), you will owe income taxes on any withdrawals.

That's the trade-off.

So why would you want to open a Traditional account if you're earning more money, and thus, are in a higher tax bracket?

To get that tax relief today.

That's the point of a Traditional account: You get a small tax relief today.

Now, there is one very important item I should note, which I have been asked *multiple* times by my clients and it's this:

You can only contribute up to the annual contribution limit among ALL of your IRA accounts.

That means you CANNOT contribute $6,500 to your Roth IRA *and* another $6,500 to your Traditional IRA in the same year (for a total of $13,000). That's *not* allowed.

But you *could* contribute $1,000 to a Roth IRA and then another $5,500 to a Traditional IRA. That's totally fine. As long as the aggregate (or total) IRA contribution does *not* exceed the annual limit (which in 2023 is $6,500).

So, let's summarize briefly what we just learned when it comes to playing the tax game.

Here are the investment accounts that can help anyone get ahead:

- Roth IRA.
- Traditional IRA.
- Roth 401k or Roth 403b.
- Individual Retirement Account.
- Traditional 401k or Traditional 403b.

I don't expect you to jump into opening every single account by tomorrow.

However, if you haven't done so already, then at least start *thinking* about the four steps we just discussed and *how* you can start building your own wealth legacy.

Challenge #12: Roth IRA versus Traditional IRA

Playing the tax game could literally save you tens of thousands – if not hundreds of thousands – of dollars over your lifetime.

I know that, because I helped the rich pay less in taxes legally during my seven years as wealth advisor at a top five wealth management company in the United States. So take it from me.

If you haven't already, it's time to start thinking about your situation right now.

The following are some questions to start turning your gears:

- How far along are you in your career?
- How far away are you from retirement?
- Can you expect to earn more money in your future years?

(Continued)

- Does your job/position have significant growth prospects?
- How much extra money can you save and invest each year?
- How much money do you plan to earn during your retirement?
- Do you plan to stay living in the United States or become an expat during retirement?

Depending on how you answer these questions, you may find that a Roth account may be more beneficial for you over a Traditional account – or vice versa.

For example, if you believe you will be in a low-income tax bracket during retirement (i.e., you won't be paying much in taxes anyway because your income will be so low), then it might make sense to open a Traditional account now and get the up-front tax benefit today. You shouldn't have to worry about paying much in taxes in the future during retirement since you don't plan to have a high income.

However, if you think you'll be in a much higher income tax bracket in the future and you're just starting your career today, then a Roth account might be the better option.

Now that you have thought a little about your current and potential future financial situation, it's time to start opening investment accounts – if you haven't already.

Opening an account is the very first step.

The next step will be to actually start investing.

And that's exactly what my next chapter will cover.

Let's jump right in.

Notes

1. Rising stocks create 300,000 new U.S. millionaires. (2 Dec. 2021). Local 3 News. https://www.local3news.com/local-news/whats-trending/rising-stocks-create-300-000-new-us-millionaires/article_93435602-a970-5aad-a881-498d8a650051.html#:~:text=(CNBC)%20%2D%2D%20The%20rising%20stock,time%20highs%20before%20the%20recession (accessed 15 July 2023).

2. Leonhardt, M. (2020). Nearly 1 in 4 millennials report having $100,000 or more in savings. [online]. CNBC. Available at: https://www.cnbc.com/2020/01/30/nearly-1-in-4-millennials-report-having-100000-or-more-in-savings.html#:~:text=In%20fact%2C%20almost%20half%20(49 (accessed 15 July 2023).

Chapter 14

Assess Your Risk Tolerance

O n the first day of my personal finance college class, I thought
I would start learning about the sexy stuff – investments.

I mean, think about it: When you hear the words *personal finance*, what picture comes *immediately* into your mind? Probably investing. Stocks. Charts. Graphs.

At least it did for me.

Believe it or not, investing is actually *not* the first thing you should think about when you have the money set aside and are ready to put it to work in the stock market.

So while I was eagerly sitting at my desk, thinking my professor would teach us about the latest inflationary trends, bull and bear market cycles, and the correlation between the market and the Consumer Price Index, I was let down. My professor did not even mention the word *investing* until about 45 minutes into class.

Instead, he talked about a little known step that happens *before* you start investing. Or at least this step *should* happen before you invest, but most often the average investor skips over this step.

It's called determining your risk tolerance.

Now, I was so confused on that first day of class, that I actually walked up to my professor after class finished and asked him if I had signed up for the wrong class. I genuinely thought personal finance would mainly focus on trading, the stock market, and investing.

He chuckled and shook his head, saying "no."

From there, he proceeded to tell me that investing is only a small percentage of personal finance.

Rather, I learned that personal finance has to do with some key factors, like understanding:
- Your future goals.
- Your risk tolerance.
- Your relationship with money.
- How you want to spend your money.
- How you are currently spending your money.

That first day of class, I learned a valuable lesson: I realized that personal finance has everything to do with your relationship with money. Investing is just like the cherry on top of a magnificently sugary sundae ice cream!

It's sexy, but the cherry (or investing in this case) *needs* to have a foundation: the ice cream, the banana, the chocolatey fudge, the sprinkles, and the whipped cream for example. In investing terms, the *foundation* represents your relationship with money.

And that's why such a large portion of this book is focused on your purpose, how you think about money, and how you treat money, rather than the actual act of *investing* your money.

I wish it were as simple as just investing in the stock market . . . and BAM! You never have to think twice about your money.

But . . . that's not exactly how it works.

We are humans, after all . . . and humans are emotional. We're not always the most logical creatures on Earth . . . that's why we fall in love, we have fits of jealousy or fits of rage. We get sad; we get happy, and so on. That's just part of what makes us *human*.

And that's great, but if you want to win with stocks, then you really should be like Spock.

I might have just given away my deep hidden secret. . . . Yes, I'm a fan of *Star Trek.* . . .

If you're not familiar with Spock, then understand that he's basically an emotionless creature who uses logic to make rational decisions. When it comes to the decision-making side of things, Spock is the complete opposite of humans.

We are FULL of emotions.

And to win with investing, we have to follow this golden rule:

Learn to control your emotions before they control you.

Now, before you read any further, I do want to clarify one key word that I'll be using often in this chapter, and probably beyond as well: *portfolio.*

When I talk about a *portfolio*, I'm actually talking about your investment portfolio. And your investment portfolio describes the number, the type, and the risk level of your investment assets. And all of these investment assets make up your portfolio.

I also want to point out two key terms we discuss in this chapter:

- Risk tolerance.
- Risk target.

Here's what those words mean, translated into plain English (you're welcome!):

Term	Defined – In Plain English
Risk Tolerance	The amount of investment risk you are willing to take without having anxiety every time there is a market drop.
Risk Target	If you were Spock (and had no emotion), this is how much risk you should be taking, given your personal factors such as your age, when you plan to retire, how much you can afford to save, and so on.

So right off the bat, you can see that the *key* difference between *risk tolerance* and *risk target* has to do with our emotions as humans.

Risk tolerance talks about the emotional stuff when it comes to investing.

Risk target, on the other hand (just like the name already implies), has to do with the Spock-like nature that we really should all employ in order to be more successful in the stock market.

The next exercise I'm going to give you is a questionnaire.

In this questionnaire, I'm going to help you figure out if you are an emotional investor or if you are a Spock-like investor.

Let's dive right in.

Your Next Steps:

Think about the March 2020 COVID-19 market drop. The market dropped to a low of 37%. Now think back to the Great Recession in 2008, where the markets dropped to a low of 51.1%. Are you vividly thinking of those volatile times? OK, now tune into your emotions. How did you feel (specifically about the stock market and any money that you may have invested during that time)?

More specifically, I want you to think about you how felt when you:

- Heard the news talking about the falling stock markets.
- Saw the value of your investments get lower and lower.
- Heard your friends talking about the falling stock markets.

. . . And most importantly, I want you to think back to *all* of those images in red that showed the Dow Jones, the S&P 500, the real estate market, and any other stock market index dropping in value rapidly.

Now that was a lot of red.

And here are the technical questions for you.

Thinking back to those volatile times, the COVID-19 and the Great Recession market crashes, what reaction *first* comes to your mind:

- Click the "sell" button and go to cash?
- Click the "buy" button to buy more stocks?
- Begin sweating like you ran 5 miles but don't do anything?

Depending on your answer, how you responded says *a lot* about you.

So, let's take some time to discuss your answers.

If you said . . .	Then it could mean . . .
Sell all positions and go to cash.	It sounds like you are a very conservative (careful) investor, whose emotions may be controlling you. Be careful and try to fight the urge to sell when markets decline.
Click "buy" to buy more stocks.	It sounds like you are a riskier investor (comfortable with stocks and the potential volatility), who is looking to buy low (when stocks are effectively "on sale"). Be careful not to dump your money into only one stock. Make sure to diversify your investments during these volatile times.
Begin sweating like you ran 5 miles but don't do anything.	It takes a lot of strength to not do anything, especially when your heart is in your mouth and you see your net worth drop lower day by day. You could take a leap of faith and buy stocks while they are so "cheap." Or, you could take the "Ostrich Approach" and simply stick your head into the sand, looking the other way during volatility (but also not giving in to your urges to "sell"). Historically speaking, every time the stock markets have dropped, the markets have also made a comeback.

Here's another question for you:
How closely do you follow the market news?

Choose from the following answers:
- Never.
- Once a week.
- Occasionally.
- CNBC Junkie.

Once again, depending on your answer, the way in which you responded says a lot about you, your investment style, and your risk tolerance.

Let me break it down for you.

If you said...	Then it could mean ...
Never.	It sounds like you probably don't care too much about how your investments are doing currently – as long as your money is in the stock market, that's all that matters. This could be a good mindset to have especially if you are a long-term investor (i.e., you need your money in the next 20+ years). A small blip on the radar today does not really hurt your long-term wealth-building goal. Often, this attitude is a winning attitude, as you take out the emotional rollercoaster that comes with investing in the stock market (since you don't see how stocks are doing on a daily basis).
Once a week.	It sounds like you want to be informed on where the market is, but you probably don't care too much where the market is every second of the day. This is also a good attitude to have when it comes to investing: you have enough knowledge to be dangerous, but you distance yourself enough to prevent any impulsive stock sells or stock buys.
CNBC Junkie.	It sounds like you may be an investing junkie. If you find yourself sweating and enraged after every time you watch or read the latest investment news, you may want to take a step back from the media. The worst thing that could happen is that you make an impulsive buy or sell after watching the news without rationally thinking through your options.

I do get concerned about the CNBC Junkies because the news typically spouts quite negative information, especially when it comes to the stock market and investing.

I mean, think about it: How many times have you heard the words "Recession" in the past 12 months in the media?

Unless you're *actually* in a recession, you're still going to hear the word on a pretty constant basis.

Why?

Because in the media, there is a saying that goes, "If it bleeds, it leads."

That means if there is bad news – even the slightest glimmer of negative news – then the media will report on it. Why? Because humans like to read bad news.

It's psychological, but it's true.

How many times do we see "happy" news? Maybe about a successful marriage, a person who landed their dream job, a family's first vacation in 10 years to their dream country?

Unfortunately, it's rare to read about "happy" news. "Happy" news isn't as much of a magnet as "negative" news. And that's why there are so many stories about bombings, fires, killings, recession fears, market crashes, and so on. Negative news leads. It attracts views.

Why am I explaining so much about the psychology behind negative news?

Because I have witnessed countless people tune into the radio, television, YouTube, or even other social media platforms where influencers share negative news about the stock market. And because these people read the negative news, they get scared. And when they get scared, they get emotional. And sadly, when humans get emotional, they don't always make the best decisions – especially when it comes to their money.

I'm not saying you should tune out the news entirely, all I'm saying is to take the news with a grain of salt. Or several grains if you can *before* making an impulse decision.

OK, enough about the news.

Let's take some time to explore your mindset when it comes to investing.

What is the *first* word that pops into your mind when you hear the word *risk*?
- Doubt.
- Danger!
- Opportunity.

Let's dissect your answer and reveal what it *truly* means.

If you said . . .	Then it could mean . . .
Doubt.	That you are uncertain about the current stock market conditions, and that you may doubt the stock market as a whole (and you may be looking for alternative investments, such as real estate, cryptocurrency, leaving everything in cash, etc.). Even if you doubt the stock market volatility, remember to focus on your long-term goals and that volatility is (historically speaking) temporary.
Danger.	You may be overly worried about stock market volatility. If you fear stock market fluctuations and believe that you may sell everything you own after a short-term drop in the stock market, be careful of your actions. Remember to remove emotions from investing and focus on the long term.
Opportunity.	You could be comfortable having a larger percentage of your net worth invested in the stock market than others. You also have a mindset where you see opportunities (when stocks are "cheap") to buy when others see the danger zone (because stocks are taking a tumble). Although no one can (and no one should) time the market, buying when stocks are low can certainly help increase your portfolio returns in the long run.

Let's move on to your ability to handle the market volatility.

If you had \$100,000 invested in the stock market and you woke up tomorrow morning to see that you lost \$50,000, or 50% of your total invested value, what's your next action?

- Sell everything you have to prevent more losses.
- Consider buying while the markets are low.
- Don't sell, but start looking for other income streams like real estate.

Let's analyze your responses.

If you said . . .	Then it could mean . . .
Sell everything you have.	You may want to consider moving a larger percentage of your net worth to bonds (more conservative). Keep in mind that although bonds don't have much volatility, they also often don't provide for high returns (like stocks do). Just remember to try and battle your impulse to sell everything you own – historically speaking, market volatility is only short term. Focus on the long term and try to ride out the market lows.
Consider buying while the markets are low.	You may be inclined to take more risk than other investors. If you see a buying opportunity during market lows, you could likely make a profit in your portfolio – as long as you stick out the lows and focus on long-term growth.

If you said . . .	Then it could mean . . .
Don't sell, but start looking for other income streams like real estate.	You may enjoy the thought of diversifying your net worth in not just the stock market but in other income-producing assets (like real estate, businesses, etc.). As long as you don't sell and hold on to your investments, you can ride out the market lows.

Now, it's time to talk about market timing.

How important is beating the market to you?
- I couldn't care less.
- It's the only reason why I invest.
- All I want is to be as good as the market.

Let's check out what each response could mean:

If you said . . .	Then it could mean . . .
I couldn't care less.	You are a passive investor (like me) who is focused on long-term growth. Historically speaking, in the long-run, markets have out-performed active day traders. If you couldn't care less, you're probably in the best position possible since you won't make emotional or impulse buys or sells. You're likely sticking with your plan and investing for the future.
It's the only reason I invest.	You may be a day trader and an investor who lives for market ups and downs. You may also not like the rest of this book because I am someone who does not necessarily encourage beating the market. (I do not believe this is a sustainable long-term growth strategy.) Read more to learn more.

If you said . . .	Then it could mean . . .
All I want is to be as good as the market.	You may want to consider investing in an index fund – which essentially tracks the market. The better the market does, the better your index fund does. The worse the market is, the worse your index fund performs. You'll never beat the market, but assuming the markets continue to grow, your index fund will also continue to grow. Note: I personally only invest in index funds myself, and I highly recommend this option.

Remember, be honest with yourself while answering these questions.

There is no right or wrong answer here.

And hopefully, this exercise helped you better understand who you are as an emotional being when it comes to investing.

Remember, there is a major difference between risk tolerance and risk target.

Now that we have discussed risk tolerance (the emotional side to investing), it's time to talk about your potential risk target (no emotions, just numbers).

Although there are so, so many factors that go into determining how much stock exposure (aka equity exposure) you should have, I'm going to stick to the easiest factor: your age.

The following are some rules-of-thumb on how to invest your portfolio, depending on your age.

If you are 45 or younger, invest as in Figure 14.1.

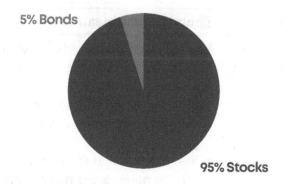

Figure 14.1

Typically speaking, it is recommended that you are 95% invested in stocks (some say to be 100% invested in stocks when you are young) and 5% invested in bonds.

When you are younger, you can afford to take more risk because you have more time to recover from economic recessions if your net worth does plummet because of the stock market.

That's why it's typically recommended to invest the majority (if not all) of your net worth in stocks – if you can handle the volatility, emotionally speaking.

If you are between 45 and 55, invest as in Figure 14.2.

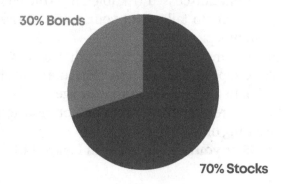

Figure 14.2

Typically, you want to dial back your risk exposure in stocks as you get older (which means you are presumably nearing retirement age, when you will need the money).

Between ages 45 and 55, you are getting closer to retirement (this is assuming the average retirement age is 65) and you cannot afford to take as much risk in your portfolio because you (and your money) don't have as much time to recover from a market downturn.

Again, this is simply an allocation target and does not mean that you *have to* invest in a 70/30 allocation.

You could certainly decrease your risk exposure (meaning you are less invested in stocks and more invested in bonds) to a 60/40 or 50/50 (or even less) allocation. What your allocation is really comes down to your own preference.

If you are 55 and older, invest as in Figure 14.3.

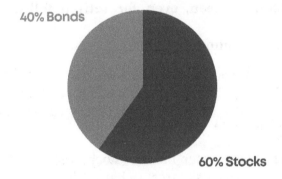

40% Bonds

60% Stocks

Figure 14.3

Again, assuming your expected retirement age is age 65, you'll likely want to continue decreasing your equity allocation (aka your risk).

I've worked with over 453 clients and I would say about 60% to 70% of those clients between the ages of 55 and 65 have a standard 60/40 portfolio (meaning 60% of their money is invested in stocks and 40% of their money is invested in bonds).

Now, let's take a look at how your equity allocation *could be* invested, if you are already in retirement.

If you are retired (regardless of age), invest as in Figure 14.4.

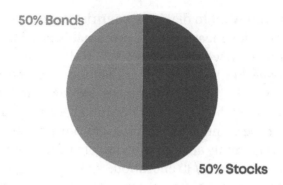

Figure 14.4

A 50/50 allocation is a common allocation for those people who are already retired.

However, the most common portfolio allocation that I have personally seen, even for retired folks, is a 60/40 allocation.

I can't say this enough:

> If you feel that you cannot handle the stock market from an emotional perspective, then it would be a good idea to consider reducing your risk (in other words, decreasing your exposure to stocks).

How you allocate your money (stocks versus bonds) simply depends on both your risk target (what we just talked about) and your risk tolerance (the emotional stuff).

Nailing your portfolio allocation is critical because the last thing you want to do is sell your stocks because you're panicking due to the stock market's volatility.

Recessions are just part of the game.

Although each recession is different (in terms of how severe it is and how long it takes to recover), one thing is certain – historically speaking: **After every recession, the market has always rebounded.**

Take a look at Figure 14.5.[1]

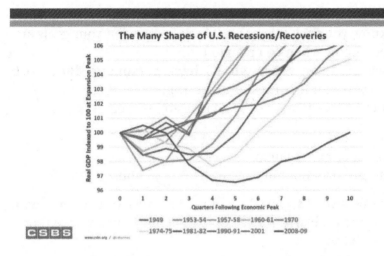

Figure 14.5
Source: www.csbs.org / @csbsnews

This chart shows three things:

1. How bad each recession was.
2. The recent and major U.S. recessions.
3. The length of time it took for each recession to recover.

The flatter the line, the longer it took for the economy to recover (like the lowest and arguably least steep line on the chart, represents the 2008–2009 recession, indicating it took the longest to recover).

If the line was steeper, this meant the recession didn't take as long to end and swing back into a bull market.

The one thing that each market downturn has in common is that after every recession, there is a recovery.

What does this mean for you and your money?

Based on historical data (and history tends to repeat itself), if you keep your money invested in the stock market (and I mean stock *market*, not just a single stock), chances are you'll see the markets (and your money) rebound in a few years (or even a few months).

So what stocks should you invest in?

Honestly, I don't think I can give you a specific answer since I don't know your risk tolerance, I don't know what your goals are, and I don't know when you plan to retire.

However, I can share what I have personally done with my money, when it comes to investing.

I believe that anyone can be an investor – whether you're:

- Young or old.
- Beginner or professional.
- Earning $10 an hour or earning $1,000 an hour.

I also believe that you don't need to invest your money with expensive and exclusive Wall Street hedge funds managers either.

Here's why:

In the long run, the markets have outperformed the average fund investor by about 6×!

The key term in this sentence is *long run*.

In the short term, yes, the average hedge fund manager could out-perform the stock market – but those profits typically don't last, especially because hedge fund managers often charge:

- 20% of profits made by the fund.
- 2% of all of the money they manage for you, regardless if they lose or make money for you.

That means you could be charged up to 22% of your money in just fees!

Here's what these hefty fees would mean for your profits: Let's say you did invest your money with a hedge fund manager. And let's say you made a 30% return that year – which is actually pretty good.

But the 30% return isn't your *net* return. It's your gross return.

What's your actual take-home *net* return?

It's 8%.

And that doesn't really sound too exciting. In fact, the S&P 500's average return over the past 50 years has hovered between 8% and 10% and that's something you could have achieved *without* hiring an expensive hedge fund manager!

So even though you could achieve high returns with hedge fund managers, their fees heavily eat into your net return, bringing the net number down.

In the finance field, the hedge fund fee rule-of-thumb is also known as the Rule of 2 and 20.

If you are OK tracking the market (aka you don't want to beat the market as most hedge fund investors do), you could simply invest *in the market* by buying a low-cost index fund.

An index fund is one fund that tracks an entire market (so even though you'd be investing in just one fund, that one fund would distribute your money across 100s if not 1,000s of companies). Index funds are the fastest, easiest, and typically the cheapest way to diversify your portfolio – which is a good thing.

For example, I personally am invested in the S&P 500 index fund (which tracks the 500 largest – and most stable – companies in America).

My S&P 500 index fund costs me about 0.04% regardless of whether I make a profit or a loss. Compare that to the potential 22% you would owe to a hedge fund manager!

Yikes!

And, if you don't believe me when I say that index funds are a great way to invest your wealth, then take it straight from the horse's mouth: Warren Buffett.

Warren Buffett, the world's 6th richest man, and arguably one of the greatest investors of our time, stated:

"I believe that 98% or 99% – maybe more than 99% – of people who invest should extensively diversify and not trade. That leads them to an index fund with very low costs."

If you don't know where to start your research when it comes to index funds, I've created the following small list of the index funds that I have personally invested in (they are low-cost and they could help diversify your investments).

Note: These index funds are my S&P 500 index fund favorites.

Fund Name	Fund Ticker Symbol	Fund Expense Ratio (aka how much it costs)	ETF or Mutual Fund
Vanguard 500 Index Fund – Admiral Shares**	VFIAX	0.040%	Mutual Fund
Vanguard 500 Index Fund	VOO	0.030%	ETF
Fidelity 500 Index Fund	FXAIX	0.015%	Mutual Fund
Schwab S&P 500 Index Fund	SWPPX	0.020%	Mutual Fund

Although this chapter simply skims the surface when it comes to investing, please keep these key points in mind when it comes to building your investment portfolio:

- Invest for the long run.
- Remember to diversify.
- Don't pick "hot" stocks.
- Don't sell during market lows.
- Invest in low-cost index funds.

To be successful investing in the stock market, you have to ride out the lows and focus on the long term.

I also want to share one more lesson when it comes to investing that could be the key to removing all emotion and help you build wealth over the long term.

This key to investing success is called: Automation, aka Dollar Cost Averaging, aka DCA.

The DCA (or dollar cost averaging strategy) is an investment strategy that automates your investments by purchasing a target asset (like an index fund) over a specific period of time (like every day, week, or month).

The reason why the DCA strategy works is because it removes your emotion when it comes to making investment decisions by automating your investments over time.

Think of the DCA strategy just like your 401k plan:

A small portion of your income is deducted and invested with every paycheck.

You don't think twice about your investments.

Similarly, the DCA strategy invests consistently, typically over decades, regardless if the markets are low or high.

The reason why this strategy works is because your emotion is removed from investing – and as you may know, emotions often can damage your investment plan (especially if you make investments on impulse . . . that's a no-no!).

Challenge #13: Think about Your Risk Tolerance and Your Risk Target

For this challenge, take some time to think about your risk tolerance (your exposure to the stock markets).

1. Consider your financial goals.
2. Consider your relationship with money.
3. Consider whether your risk target (logic) matches your risk tolerance (emotions).
4. Consider if you want to pursue an automatic dollar cost averaging (DCA) strategy.
5. Consider how you plan to invest in stocks – either with index funds (my preference) or with individual stocks.

Remember this

Anyone can be an investor – you don't have to hire a private Wall Street hedge fund manager to invest your money.

(Continued)

Here are the keys to building a successful investment portfolio:

- Invest for the long term.
- Start investing as early as possible.
- Stay consistent with your investment strategy.
- Determine your risk tolerance and make adjustments when necessary.

Even if the stock market crashes, chances are the markets will recover (at least that's how it has been every time, in the past). So, stick with the program and remember that this is a long-term play.

Note

1. The shape of things to come: Reverse radical recovery. (n.d.). Conference of State Bank Supervisors (CSBS). https://www.csbs.org/newsroom/shape-things-come-reverse-radical-recovery (accessed 15 July 2023).

Chapter 15
The Eighth Wonder of the World

We've all heard that there are Seven Wonders of the World . . . but what if I told you there are actually *eight* world wonders . . . .

And even better: what if I told you that you can see the Eighth World Wonder? . . . Every. Single. Day.

In fact, it was Albert Einstein who first coined it the Eighth World Wonder.

Any guesses?

It's called *compound interest*.

Before we jump into what compound interest actually is, let's back it up a little.

First, let's talk about investing and why so many people think investing is scary and [gasp] uncool to talk about with others.

That's a question I started asking myself when I went to high school.

Going to high school in the United States, you are exposed to a "social ranking" system for the first time in your life.

In my high school you had the:

- Cool kids.
- Nerdy kids.
- Average kids.

And typically speaking, every high school kid wants to be in the cool crowd.

I certainly did.

In my high school, you were considered to be in the cool crowd if you bought the newest clothes, followed the latest trends, and knew the latest gossip.

The second you failed to deliver, you'd be removed from the cool crowd. It wasn't easy to get back in, either.

Trust me, talking about investing in high school (like I did) was definitely *not* what the cool crowd did (and that's why I was never considered "cool").

And that high school experience – trying to impress others for status or recognition – might actually stick with some of us far past our high school years.

Think about it: So many people want to impress others who really don't care . . .

The one thing that 100% of the population cares about is themselves. That's just human nature.

So why even bother trying to be "popular" by "fitting in" and impressing others who don't even care in the first place?

I see this with so many other adults in the "real world" – outside of high school.

For example, the other day, I was helping a client organize his budget. His numbers were WAY off, as he was overspending by about $1,000 per MONTH.

That's about $12,000 per year . . . and if he wanted to build any long-term wealth, then he would have to act fast and reduce his expenses.

You want to know what the No. 1 thing was that he spent money on?

Designer clothes. Yep.

This former client earned about $50,000 per year and was in absolutely no place to spend $5,000 on a designer backpack (which, for the record, he did against my suggestion).

That designer backpack is worth one-tenth of his overall gross annual salary – and doesn't even take into account his annual *net* salary after taxes are taken out.

Scratching my head in bewilderment, I asked my client, "Why do you need a $5,000 luxury backpack? Don't you already have a backpack that has the same function?"

He looked at me like I had five heads and three arms!

After recovering from the shock of hearing my (apparently) ludicrous question, he gave me his answer: "Fiona, I have a group of friends and to fit in, those designer items *are* my look."

Now, it was my turn to look at him in disbelief.

Maybe he was in the wrong circle of friends if they required him to own luxury clothes to be a part of their group.

I may have come across as harsh, but someone had to tell him.

There was no way that I could sugarcoat the situation. If he continued spending $12,000 over his annual *gross* income, then retirement (which was a major goal of his) would not be an option, at least not at the current spending and income level.

So what's the lesson here?

If you fit in, you'll be easily controlled.

And those who are controlled don't dare to think outside of the box.

They aim for safety and security rather than taking a calculated risk and opportunity – especially when they are young.

Sadly, schools don't teach us these vital life lessons (at least mine didn't) – and that's why you need to read this book – and pass it on to your kids so they learn these vital life lessons early.

With that said, let's jump into the Eighth World Wonder.

Enter compound interest.

The Power of Compound Interest

If you harness the power of compound interest from an early age by investing and continuing to invest consistently over time, there is SUCH a high chance that you will become a millionaire.

The key is that you start early.

Because *time* is the most important ingredient when taking full advantage of compound interest.

In fact, about 75% of investors regret not having started earlier.[1]

Why?

The earlier you invest, the MUCH higher the chance you become a millionaire.

And it all comes down to the *time IN the market*, not *timing the market*.

The more time you spend in the market, the more you can harness the power of compound interest.

Compound interest, in plain English, is the phenomenon where your money is earning you more money.

Technically speaking, compound interest is when you earn interest on top of your interest because you are reinvesting your interest.

Simply put:

- You won't see a big change in your investment in the beginning with compound interest.
- In 20 to 40 years from now, though, you'll see the magnitude of the impact of compound interest.

The key to compound interest is patience (aka time).

It takes time to see the impact of compound interest, which is why you should start investing as early as possible.

Here's another good summary of what compound interest is, in the words of Albert Einstein:

"Compound interest is the 8th wonder of the world. He who understands it, earns it. He who doesn't, pays it."

And for that exact reason, I wanted to take some time to talk about the true power of compound interest so you know why this chapter is so important: **Start investing now.**

Shockingly, however, 43% of Millennials are not investing[2] . . . which is a major problem.

Try asking your friends – regardless of their age – about investing. Chances are, they're not investing yet – or they may have started at some point but are not continuing to invest.

You might even get excuses that could vary from:

- "I'll invest tomorrow."
- "I haven't had time to start."
- "I don't know which stocks to buy."
- "I don't make enough money to invest."

The excuse that irks me the most is "I haven't had time to start." Everyone has time, 24 hours, to be exact. I'm not sure why people still believe that the only way you can start investing is with $1,000s of dollars. You can invest even with just $5! Sometimes even less.

It's called fractional investing, and many online apps offer fractional investing as an option. *Fractional investing* gives you the option to invest in actual stocks, but only for a *fraction* of the price of one stock.

Here's an example: At the time that I was writing this book, the price of one Amazon stock cost $130.36. Now, not everyone has a spare $130.36 sitting around. That's a lot of money, especially if you're just starting out in your investing journey. It's understandable.

Now, not even 10 years ago, if you wanted to invest in Amazon, you would have had to fork up exactly $130.36 to buy into one share. Not anymore. As of around 2017, investing in stocks was made much easier for the everyday investor (like you and me). Now, you can invest in just a fraction of the Amazon stock, thanks to fractional investing.

So, instead of coughing up the full $130.36 to buy into Amazon, you can *still* become an owner of Amazon stock for just a few dollars! Maybe that's $5. Maybe that's $10. Whatever you can invest. Some platforms might have investment minimums (e.g., that could be $5), so just make sure you check out those minimums first.

The new-age fractional investing applications can be accessed on your desktop computer or even on your iPhone.

There are even some applications that are called *micro-investing platforms*. They specialize in helping people invest a few dollars of their money into the stock market so at least people can start taking advantage of the power of compound interest.

And the best part is that not only can you start investing with just a few dollars, but you also don't have to understand everything there is about investing. That's why there are apps called robo-advisors, which can help guide you through making investment decisions.

For example, robo-advisors can put you into an asset allocation and manage that asset allocation for you – so you don't ever have to reallocate that portfolio or rebalance the portfolio as the markets fluctuate over time.

Believe it or not, you don't need to pick stocks to win.

You can win if you invest in a low-cost index fund and hold your investment for the long term (investing legends such as Warren Buffett, Charlie Munger, and Rakesh Jhunjhunwala would agree with this idea).

In fact, let me tell you a story that I first heard about back in high school.

And, yes, over a decade later, that story has stuck with me.

It's about a chimpanzee and a Wall Street investor.

And, yes, it's a true story.

So many people believe that in order to be successful at finance, you have to invest. And in order to be successful with investing, you have to hire the best investment professionals with Ivy League degrees who work in massive hedge funds, on Wall Street or at nationally recognized investment management firms.

Well, guess what?

They're all wrong.

What would you say if I told you that a chimpanzee managed to out-perform both the Wall Street experts *and* the S&P 500?

Keep reading.

It all started in 1973, when a Princeton University professor named Burton Malkiel (the author of *A Random Walk Down Wall Street*) claimed that a blindfolded monkey throwing darts at random companies would create an investment portfolio that would perform just as well – if not better – than a carefully curated investment portfolio managed by professionals.

The bet was on.

And the bet involved Raven, a six-year-old chimpanzee.

Raven was given darts to actually throw at a list of companies. In fact, she created her own portfolio with exactly 133 companies. In effect, Raven created her own index, which was later dubbed the MonkeyDex (yes, it's a true story!).[3]

How do you think the MonkeyDex performed?

Let's just say that Raven's MonkeyDex out-performed more than 6,000 professional hedge fund and investment management professionals on Wall Street. Reread that sentence again.

You read that right.

In fact, that year, which was 1999, Raven the Chimpanzee became the 22nd most successful money manager in the United States. A monkey.

And what was Raven's strategy?

Randomly throwing darts at a list of companies to create the MonkeyDex. In fact, in 1999, Raven gained 213% in her portfolio![4]

So what's the moral of this story?

You don't need to hire a fancy investment professional to manage your portfolio. In fact, you do it yourself.

While I'm not saying you should go running into the basement, start dusting off your old dartboard, and stick random company names on the dartboard, I *am* saying that you can create an investment portfolio that can do as well or better than the S&P 500. And take advantage of the power of compound interest.

Now, I personally am a lazy investor.

I don't like thinking twice about my investment decisions – let alone day trade. Ugh.

So what do I do? I let the index do the work for me.

Yes, I know, I'll never out-perform the markets that way, but investing in an index (which could be the S&P 500 index, the Bloomberg Aggregate Bond Index, the Russell 2000 Index, etc.) does the work for me. It frees up my time to do the things that really matter – like work on my business, spend time with family, or just chill out.

Now, I know what some of you might be thinking: the year in which Raven the Chimpanzee's experiment was conducted, 1999, was part of the dot-com era (and bubble). Yes. You are 100% correct.

So, in theory, it would have been pretty difficult for Raven to create a losing MonkeyDex since the stock market was soaring to all-time highs until the dot-com bubble burst in 2000.

So let me give another example for all you nay-sayers to prove my point that you – yes, you – can successfully build your own investment portfolio.

This time, we'll take a look at the company Research Affiliates. This company mimicked Raven's actions using computer technology (without actually using a monkey). In this experiment, Research Affiliates randomly created 100 portfolios. Each portfolio contained 30 random stocks chosen from a list of 1,000 companies.

The 1,000 companies represented an index (similar to the S&P 500 index, which represents 500 companies).

Research Affiliates included one additional factor where Raven the Chimpanzee's experiment failed: Research Affiliates repeated this process (generating 100 portfolios with 30 stocks each) across a 47-year time frame, ranging from 1964 to 2010.[5]

Adding the element of a timeframe into the experiment that would encapsulate recessions like the 2000 dot-com recession, the 2008 Great Recession, and so on, could help drive home the idea that a random portfolio could, in fact, beat Wall Street managers.

Any guesses on the results?

An unbelievable 98% of the "monkey portfolios" beat the returns of the 1,000 company index each year. Yes, 98% of them.

My goal isn't to encourage you to pick up your things and drive down to the local pet store to buy your newest dart-throwing monkey. Quite the contrary. I just want to give you a pinch of reassurance that you don't need a human – or an animal – to help you create your portfolio.

Invest in an index fund portfolio. Set it and forget it. And automate your investment contributions so, over time, you can take advantage of the imperious power of compound interest. Of course, as you have life events or get closer to certain life events (like marriage, divorce, retirement, death, etc.), check back into your allocation and readjust it as necessary.

It really doesn't take a genius (refer back to Raven the Chimpanzee's story) to become successful when investing in the stock market.

So save yourself the money. Don't try to beat the market using fancy technology and tools. Most of the time, that won't be worth your money or time. Yes, maybe you'll beat the market over the short term. But there's a pretty low chance you'll beat the market over the long term.

The key is to leverage the *time IN the market* that you have left to fully take advantage of compound interest.

Challenge #14: Harnessing the Eighth Wonder of the World

This chapter primarily focused on the power of compound interest and how everyone – including YOU – can take advantage of it now.

The key, though, to truly harnessing that Eighth world wonder is time.

And remember the saying "what matters is time IN the market and not timing the market." If anything, the two previous examples, first with Raven the Chimpanzee and

(Continued)

second with the company Research Affiliates, should have supported this.

Now that you hopefully have a little more confidence in your own ability to win financially, here are your next steps:

- If you have not opened an investment account yet, now is the time to do so.
- Before you open an account though, make sure you think about which platform you want to use: A micro-investing platform (if you're not ready to put $100s or $1,000s into investing just yet); a robo-advisor platform (if you want and need the guidance); a traditional broker-age platform (like Fidelity or Charles Schwab, if you are comfortable working and managing your own money).
- Think about how *much* you can start contributing.
- Think about *when* you can contribute (the first of every month? Twice a month? And so on).
- Think about *what* investments you will contribute to (an index fund? If so, which one or ones? The S&P 500? The Bloomberg Bond Aggregate Index fund? The Emerging Market Index Fund? And so on).

I want you to take advantage of the next hour or so, while this material is still fresh in your mind, to write down – on paper – the answers to the preceding five bullet points.

Invest the time in yourself and in your future TODAY.

You will thank me later.

Notes

1. Stobierski, Tim. (19 Dec. 2022). Most investors wish they got started sooner. [online]. Grow with Acorns. https://grow.acorns.com/most-investors-wish-they-got-started-sooner/#:~:text=Nearly%20one%2Dthird%20(31%25),45%20years%20away%20from%20retirement (accessed 15 July 2023).

2. Doyle, Karen. (27 June 2019). 43% of Millennials aren't investing, survey finds. [online]. Yahoo! Video. https://www.yahoo.com/video/43-millennials-arent-investing-090000387.html#:~:text=Specifically%2C%2043%25%20of%20millennials%20aren,them%20accomplish%20their%20financial%20goals (accessed 10 July 2023).

3. Most successful chimpanzee on Wall Street. (n.d.). Guinness World Records. https://www.guinnessworldrecords.com/world-records/most-successful-chimpanzee-on-wall-street (accessed 1 July 2023).

4. Most successful chimpanzee on Wall Street. (n.d.). Guinness World Records. https://www.guinnessworldrecords.com/world-records/most-successful-chimpanzee-on-wall-street (accessed 1 July 2023).

5. Tayal, Puja. (4 Aug. 2021). Monkey beats stock market. [online]. Yahoo! Finance Canada. https://ca.finance.yahoo.com/news/monkey-beats-stock-market-172803113.html#:~:text=According%20to%20a%202012%20Forbes,large%20portion%20of%20the%20market (accessed 1 July 2023).

Chapter 16
Become a Master Budgeter

As a college kid who was working full-time on the side, I really struggled to make ends meet.

College was expensive – even though I wasn't attending any fancy, private college. I mean, who charges $800 for an economics book? Each class I was taking cost between $3,000 and $5,000.

And in between loading up on homework, projects, and extra credit, I also had to make sure I made enough money to pay for my rent, food, tuition, car pass, and so on. While I cherish those times because I certainly learned to never take money for granted, it was not easy. At all.

I practically lived on Ramen noodle soup.

While I certainly learned a lot from my college degree, I think I could have learned a lot of the topics for free online. I mean, you have YouTube, you have Udemy, Coursera, and so on. There are *so* many incredible sources out there all for free – or at minimum, they cost less than what I paid to the college.

And I don't know why everyone told me that college would be the "best four years of my life" because my college years were probably some of the most stressful years of my life.

In fact, I wanted to get out of college as fast as possible. To keep me motivated, I kept a vision board in my dorm room. And on that vision board, I tracked the number of days I had left of college classes. I remember at one point that number exceeded 500 days . . . and ever so slowly, that relatively large number started creeping down.

Because I wanted to get out of college as fast as possible, I took as many classes in one semester as the college regulations permitted (yes, there was a maximum number of classes you could take within one semester). After 2.5 years of hard work, I managed to graduate. And I was out of there, ready to jump-start the real world.

At age 21, I said "hasta la vista" and entered the workforce.

Although I found that my college classes really didn't seem to teach me any substantial life knowledge, my 2.5 years at college taught me something that no other class could have: **How to Budget – For Real Life**.

I'm not saying that an actual *class* at college prepared me to budget for real life.

But my entire college experience – from working 40-hour weeks on top of taking the maximum number of college class to bartering with bookstores to lower the cost of a single college textbook – really helped open my eyes to what *real life* is like.

In fact, it was thanks to my college experience that I learned some valuable lessons like learning how to start and KEEP a budget.

Now, I didn't even take a budgeting class. My teacher was life. And sometimes, life is the best teacher out there.

In fact, have you ever typed into Google "best budgeting technique" or "how to budget?"

Well, let me tell you that there are 100s of different blog posts on budgeting, each telling its own story or version on how to make your finances follow a specific budget.

I've seen so many different budgeting formulas out there, like the:
- 70-20-10 budget.
- 50-30-20 budget.
- Zero-based budget.
- Envelope system budget.
- Pay yourself first budget.

And the list goes on.

Basically, every one of these budget rules tells you how much you should budget for monthly living expenses, savings, and "fun money."

Yet, I find that none of these budgets really help guide you on *how much* you should be spending on the biggest chunk of your expenses: Rent. Or, *how much* you should be spending on debt, like credit card or car debt.

To be successful with your financial picture, you have to imagine that you are the Household CFO – the family Chief Financial Officer.

You'll have to know exactly:
- How your money is spent.
- On what your money is spent.
- How much money is coming into your bank account.
- How much money is going out of your bank account.
- Why your money is being spent (is it a need, want, wish?).
- If you are running a deficit (more is going out than is coming in).
- If you are running a surplus (more is coming in than is going out).

You *have* to know everything there is to know about your money – or else it's so easy to lose track of it.

And oddly enough, I know SO many people who don't like looking at their numbers. They don't *want* to know how much they are spending on eating out, vacation, clothes, or whatever it is.

These types of people are ostriches. They stick their head in the sand and don't want to be bothered by what is actually happening. These types of people prefer to walk around blindly with little to no knowledge about their financial situation.

Is this you?

Be honest.

If it is, then think about it this way: Let's say you're just preparing for a long race. Maybe you've been training for a marathon. Or maybe it's just a casual stroll in the park. Either way, would you start running with a blindfold?

If you have a blindfold, you will have ZERO idea of where you are going and what is happening in front of you.

You would just blindly "hope" that everything goes OK. That you don't crash into a tree. Fall over a rock. Or trip someone else by accident.

Running or walking with a blindfold will not help you reach your goal.

The same goes to avoiding your finances.

And it's time to rip off that blindfold. NOW.

If you want to BUILD your wealth, then it's time to start looking into the numbers. Into your budget. And into your net worth.

Yes, this might be a little dirty. A little painful. And not a lot of fun. But, it's necessary. Again, if you want to win your race – whether that means saving enough money to go on a vacation or paying off your debt or retiring early – you need to first understand your situation.

And understanding your situation starts by understanding your numbers.

So what does that even mean? Understanding your numbers?

To me, that means two things:

- Understanding your budget.
- Understanding your net worth.

We'll go over these two items in this chapter.

But first, I want to assure you that numbers are NOT intimidating. They are just numbers, after all. They're not going to bite you or hurt you or scare you. In fact, numbers are like the shining beam coming from a flashlight. They illuminate the path for you.

Maybe the numbers aren't exactly what you want to see, but they will help pave the path for you and they'll help guide you into the right direction.

If you're REALLY not a numbers person, then here's my trick for you: make it fun.

In fact, why don't you put down this book right now and do the following:

- Prepare your favorite snack.
- Pour yourself a glass of your favorite drink.
- Put on some relaxing, chill music for background ambiance.

The trick is to create a low-key environment.

Especially if you're already hesitant and intimidated by numbers, you don't want your environment to pile on more stress. That's why every time I start my budget, I pour myself a glass of red wine and I have a plate of my favorite cheeses. It's actually something I look forward to!

In fact, for this week, I want you to take out your calendar right now. Whether it's your digital calendar or your physical calendar. Now, find a date and time where you can schedule exactly one hour of your time to review your numbers. Your budget.

I'm serious. This is going to help.

Now, during this timeframe, it's up to you to figure out what's going on in your money life.

We're going to try to answer some of the following questions:

- How much are you spending?
- How much are you making?
- Where is the money going?

Typically speaking, you'll have access to your spending numbers thanks to the many tools that are available and typically integrated with your banking and credit card software.

So here are some examples that have worked for me personally in the past:

- Your credit card spend analyzer.
- Your checking/banking account budget tool.
- Any linked budgeting apps you're currently using.

Typically speaking, credit cards offer built-in spend analyzers that take note of your entire transactional history. Not only that, but these spend analyzers also categorize your spending for you. So for example, an expense at McDonald's would be automatically categorized under the "Dining Out" category. Or a purchase of an airline ticket would be automatically categorized under "Travel." The spend analyzers also typically calculate your monthly average spending. This monthly average helps you see whether you were "above" or "below" your average spending.

Most modern credit cards should have access to a spend analyzer like this either on the mobile app or when you log into your desktop online portal. If you don't see a spend analyzer, then I would give customer service a call to see if they can guide you to the right location.

If your credit card does not have a spend analyzer, the next step is to consider your bank. I would not only check out your bank's desktop version but I would also download the mobile application for your bank.

Chances are, your bank will offer a mobile app that tracks your spending (at least as it is withdrawn from your checking or savings accounts). For example, one of the banks I personally have used in the past, Chase, offers this money tracking feature when you download its banking application on your mobile phone.

From there, you can accurately see your monthly income (assuming you receive direct deposits into your bank account) and your monthly expenses (assuming your expenses are directly withdrawn from your bank account and not just your credit card). However, I do know that not every bank offers such a tracking app for its checking account.

And if that's not the case, then I would also check to see if you have any active budgeting apps that you could use to help create your budget.

A great budgeting app like YNAB (aka You Need a Budget) helped me track every dollar and made sure I never overspent again (YNAB is free for students and offers a 34-day free trial to everyone else).

If you're not willing to pay money for a budgeting app, then you may even want to try out free budgeting resources. As an example, the Mint budgeting app by Intuit is free (at least the base version) and can help you track your income and expenses accordingly.

And, if you prefer to keep everything in house instead of linking your credit cards and debit cards to an external budgeting app, then of course, your old-fashioned Excel (or Numbers, if you're an Apple user) will do the trick as well.

Now, keep in mind that budgeting isn't just some boring task.

Budgeting is a life-planning tool. In fact, it makes your life goals a reality.

In fact, I want you to visualize this scenario:

Let's say that you are planning a 3,000-mile road trip from California to Florida. That's a long distance; you're pretty much going from one end of the country to the other. Would you be able to travel 3,000 miles without looking at a single map?

Perhaps you have superhuman navigation skills. I definitely do not.

I would NEED a map to help navigate me from Point A to Point B. Your budget is your roadmap.

Budgeting Rules of Thumb

Now that you know *how* to budget, let's actually figure out some of the top budgeting rules of thumb. I wanted to give you a snapshot of the four key rules that you need to know if your goal is to "make it" in life.

In fact, these very four rules of thumb are pretty much the same rules of thumb that the 453 millionaires I've worked with in the past have used as well to build – and maintain – their fortunes.

Type of Expense	Rule of Thumb	Gross vs. Net
Monthly Housing Debt	< 28% of gross monthly income	Gross
Total Monthly Consumer Debt	< 20% of net monthly income	Net
Total Monthly Debt Payments	< 36% of gross monthly income	Gross
Retirement & Savings Contributions	≥ 20% or more of gross monthly income	Gross

These rules of thumb are not just created out of thin air. In fact, these rules are precise numbers that are recommended by the prestigious Certified Financial Planner® Board, which is a nationally recognized top financial institution.

By combing through thousands of pieces of real-life data, the CFP® Board has developed these rules and recommended them to their clients, CFP® practitioners, and the everyday person.

Before we break down the bigger meaning of this chart, I think first you need to understand the difference between two key terms: *net income* and *gross income*.

Net income is the total amount of money you can actually spend, after paying for taxes, Social Security, and other deductions.

Gross income, on the other hand, is the total amount of money you actually earn, before taxes, Social Security, and so on are taken out of your paycheck.

Now that you know the difference between net income – your actual take home pay – versus gross income – let's break down my four basic budgeting rules into bite-sized information.

Rule 1: Monthly Housing Debt

First, I think it's important to take a look at how much you should be spending on your monthly housing debt (or rent, if you don't own a home).

Rule of Thumb	Description
Housing Debt	< 28% of gross monthly income

In other words, you want to spend *less than* 28% of your gross (total) monthly income on housing debt.

Housing debt could include all of the following:
- Taxes.
- Interest.
- Principal.

- Insurance.
- Homeowners' Association fees.

The shocking part is that about 40 million Americans spend more than 30% of their income on housing payments. That's a BIG chunk of money.[1]

Honestly, I find that *a lot* of people buy more house than they need and/or can afford.

So before you buy that new house or sign the lease on a new, lofty apartment, I want you to really think about how much living space you need.

Chances are, you probably don't need the extra room or the extra addition.

In fact, the average American living in the United States back in the 1950s owned a house that was less than 1,000 square feet in size. In present times, the average American house is now about 2,500 square feet – or more! To make matters even more interesting, about 70 years ago, Americans needed only about 300 square feet of house to live, while in 2023 and beyond, the average person needs about 1,000 square feet to live.[2]

In the 1950s, people didn't need so much space. But for some reason, the modern American requires more and more space. In fact, based on these numbers, the average space per person has more than tripled!

That's where the question begs: is all that space *really* necessary?

The answer is probably "no."

More space isn't always better, either.

Here are some reasons why:

- The smaller the space, the easier to clean.
- The smaller the space, the cheaper the cost of rent or mortgage.
- The smaller the space, the easier to move out.
- The smaller the space, the lower the heating and cooling costs.

Overall, you're probably better off keeping your living space small and not opting for the biggest house (or apartment) on your block.

Save yourself the money and instead invest it for your future retirement, pay off debt, build up your emergency savings fund, or maybe spend a little bit on yourself too, once in a while!

Of course, it's not as easy as just saying "spend less than 28% of your gross monthly income on housing costs."

I get it.

I'm living in this world as well. Inflation is rampant. Wages are largely stagnant. Everything costs more – sometimes double or even triple – than what it used to cost. I have eyes and ears too.

What I'm trying to say is that this is *just* a rule of thumb. It's not set in stone.

And if you find yourself overspending on rent (at least for now), there are ways to make your situation better.

For example, you could:

- Find a new job.
- Find new side hustles.
- Find a roommate to split costs.

If you own a house, you may also want to consider refinancing your mortgage.

Of course, whether that's a good idea (or not) depends on several factors:

- Your current interest rate.
- The new interest rate you could lock in.
- How long you plan to stay living in your house.

If you plan to move out of your house within five years or less of the refinance, then it typically doesn't make sense to refinance your home.

The reason why is because of what's called a "closing cost."

Closing costs are typically expenses and various fees associated with refinancing. Of course, the banks aren't going to refinance your mortgage for free, right?

And depending on the state you live in, these closing costs may range anywhere from a few hundred dollars to a few thousand dollars.

As an example, when I lived in Florida and refinanced my old house from 4.375% to a 3% interest rate, which was a big win for me and saved me about $400 per month, I had to pay about $7,000 just in closing costs.

Now, you don't have to panic, because closing costs (unless you have the extra cash on the sidelines) are typically rolled into your refinance.

This means if you are refinancing a $200,000 mortgage and incur $5,000 of closing fees for the refinance, your total new loan balance (after the closing costs are rolled into your refinance) would be $205,000.

You don't have to pay out of pocket, but you do have to pay in the future.

The ideal situation, if you want to refinance your mortgage, is to lower your interest rate by *a minimum of 50 basis points.*

What are basis points?

Basis points are essentially hundredths of a percent. As an example, 1 percent or 1.00% is equal to 100 basis points. On the other hand, 50 basis points is equal to 0.50% or one-half of a percent.

And lowering your mortgage interest rate by 50 basis points or more, would be a good deal when considering refinancing. But, if your current interest rate is 3.5% then it probably doesn't make sense to refinance to a 3.25% interest rate.

Lowering your interest rate would also help lower how much you pay toward housing costs.

However, I offer a word of caution:

Make sure to triple-check the financing terms of your refinance so that the terms don't catch you off-guard (e.g., you may expect a different interest rate if you are obtaining a balloon loan payment over a 30-year fixed loan payment). These are two very different mortgages and you want to triple-check whether you are entering into the right deal for yourself.

If done correctly, however, refinancing your mortgage interest rate could help lower your expenses by several hundred dollars a month – which could make a big difference over the long run.

Rule 2: Total Monthly Debt Payments

Next, let's take a look at how much you should be spending on total monthly debt payments.

Rule of Thumb	Description
Total Monthly Debt Payments	< 36% of gross monthly income

In other words, you want to spend *less than* 36% of your gross (total) monthly income on total monthly debt payments.

Debt payments could include all of the following

- Car loan payments.
- Mortgage payments.
- Credit card payments.
- Student loan payments.

If you find yourself spending more than 36% of gross monthly income on total debt payments, I strongly recommend you create a budget, cut out unnecessary expenses, and actually stick to it.

A good way to start cutting your expenses if you find yourself spending more than the recommended 36% of gross monthly income is by categorizing your spending into three sections:

- Your Needs.
- Your Wants.
- Your Wishes.

Your needs are your nonnegotiable daily living expenses. In other words, you need to spend that money to live.

Some typical expenses that would be categorized as a "need" would include:

- Rent.
- Food.
- Medical insurance.

Of course, you don't want to *overspend* on rent or food, for example, either.

Wants, on the other hand, are things that you would *like* to have but don't need to keep yourself and your family alive.

Examples of "wants" purchases include:

- Eating out.
- A newer car.
- A new dress when you already have one.

These are all "nice to have" purchases, but again, they are not required to keep you alive.

And finally, the "wishes" expense category would encompass any spending on those lofty, dream goals we all have.

Below are some examples of "wishes" expenses:

- A fancy vacation.
- Buying a new home.
- Donating money to charity.

As you can see, the expenses in the "wishes" category are a little bit loftier, more expensive, and possibly have a longer time frame until you can accomplish them (unless you inherit a gigantic amount of money in the interim to splurge on these goals).

Now that you've categorized your expenses into these three categories, it's time to slash your spending in the "wishes" and the "wants" categories.

If you feel like this is too big of a move for you right now – that's OK.

Start out by cutting at least one expense in the "wishes" or "wants" categories. Even if that expense is just $1. I don't care.

Why?

Because you're building a *habit*. And as it is widely known, a habit can take anywhere from 20 to 60 days or more to form. As long as you are starting to categorize and cut your spending one-by-one, you are already on the right track to become a master budgeter.

Rule 3: Total Consumer Debt Payments

Now it's time to review how much you should be spending on total consumer debt payments.

Rule of Thumb	Description
Total Consumer Debt Payments	< 20% of net monthly income

In other words, you want to spend less than 20% of your *net monthly income* (total income minus taxes, Social Security, etc.).

Consumer debt payments may include all of the following
- Lines of credit.
- Cash advances.
- Credit card debt.

As you may have guessed, the most common type of consumer debt is the credit card.

In fact, about 35% of Americans carry an existing credit card debt balance.[3]

That means 1 out of every 3 Americans will have existing credit card debt. That number has ticked up by about 6% from 2022.[4]

It makes sense, too. We've had COVID-19. We've had millions of people losing their jobs. We've had record-high inflation. We've had stagnating wages. And so much more.

Life isn't easy.

But let me tell you one thing: if there is *anything* you are learning from this book, I implore you to crush your credit card debt as fast as possible.

You *do not* want to carry consumer debt – and that's because most consumer debt (specifically credit card debt) happens to be high-interest debt (typically interest rates are north of 20%).

Rule 4: Retirement and Savings Contributions

It's important to realize that your savings and investment contributions also are a part of your budget.

Rule of Thumb	Description
Total Retirement & Savings	20% or more of gross monthly income

Now that 20% number might take you by surprise.

Most financial "gurus" say to save around 10% to 15% of your monthly income for retirement . . . but I don't exactly agree with that number.

Saving between 10% to 15% of your income won't really get you too far – especially thanks to the following:

- Inflation.
- Longer lifespans.
- Stagnating wages.
- Increased cost of living.
- Increased health care costs.

Saving 10% to 15% of your income won't cut it anymore.

This rule is outdated to be honest.

Especially if your goal is to retire early, become a millionaire in the next few years, or bulk up your investment accounts, you shouldn't just follow the "average" rule of thumb.

If you want to be above average, then you have to do what the average person will not.

To do more in your future, you have to do more in your present.

That's why I would recommend saving and/or investing *at a minimum* 20% of your net income (total income minus taxes, Social Security, etc.).

And I'll be honest with you: even 20% is not enough.

I almost wrote "save 30%," but decided to stick with 20% for now in an effort to not shock my readers. Because saving and investing a minimum of 30% of your income can be difficult, which I understand.

Personally, however, I take these saving and investing rules as a challenge. And I *love* challenges.

In fact, this past year, I upped my savings and investment rate from 65% to 70% of my income.

Here's how I manage to save 70% of my income
- Use coupons.
- Go thrift shopping.
- Grow my own food.
- Increase my income.
- Sell stuff I don't need.
- Decrease my expenses.
- Negotiate my utility bills.

Trust me, it's not easy for me to stick to a rigid plan and save 70% of my income.

But, I keep reminding myself that, in order to win in the future, you have to give up a little bit today.

Now keep in mind these are simply budgeting rules of thumb. If you find yourself overspending in one category, try to trim back your spending in another category to balance out your budget.

In the end, finance is more of an art than a science. And it's all about balance.

Especially if you are new to budgeting – please do not stress out if you find yourself paying more than these rules of thumb recommend.

No one expects you to be perfect – remember that perfection is an illusion – and no one expects you to completely change your financial picture within 24 hours.

The most important thing is that you start today, you start small, and you progressively move toward your financial goals – whatever those might be.

Your Net Worth

If you remember from earlier in this chapter, I talked about understanding the numbers. And more specifically, I talked about understanding both your budget numbers and your net worth numbers.

So, let's briefly talk about your net worth.

Your net worth essentially tracks how much money you are (or aren't) worth.

Here's the actual net worth formula:

Net Worth = Assets – Liabilities

As a quick refresher, assets are all of the things that you *own* or at minimum they are the things in which you have equity.

Here are some examples of common assets:

- Cash.
- Jewelry.
- Retirement accounts.
- The equity part of your house.

Liabilities are the exact opposite of assets. Liabilities are all the debts that you owe to the bank, to a company, or to a person in some cases.

Here are some common examples of liabilities:

- Car loans.
- Mortgages.
- Credit cards.

Ideally, you'll want to get rid of your liabilities over time. They drag down your net worth.

Typically, there are three net worth outcomes:

- You have a negative net worth.
- You have a positive net worth.
- You have a $0 net worth.

Having a positive net worth means you're already ahead of the curve. That means you own more than what you owe. Now it's important to understand that a positive net worth doesn't necessarily mean that you have $0 in liabilities. It just means that what you own (your assets) outnumber your liabilities (what you owe).

If you have a positive net worth but still have credit card debt – that's not exactly a great place to be. You should prioritize getting rid of your credit card debt as fast as possible.

Having a $0 net worth is actually pretty good as well. A lot of people I coach think that a $0 net worth is a bad thing, when in reality, it's not! It means that what you own is as much as what you owe. Or, it might mean that you don't owe anything (and you don't own anything either).

With a $0 net worth, you know that a positive net worth is right around the corner!

And finally, if you have a negative net worth, that's also not necessarily a bad thing. But it certainly means you have some work to do.

Now, before you start panicking, the very first thing I would do if I had a negative net worth is to actually understand the *types* of liabilities I have.

For example, do I have:

- Car debt?
- Mortgage debt?
- Credit card debt?

If it turns out I have a negative net worth just because of my mortgage debt, I really wouldn't be too concerned. That's because mortgage debt is considered "smart debt." It's debt that is associated with an appreciating asset (your house).

And typically speaking, mortgage debt has a lower interest than bad debt, like credit card debt.

However, if your net worth is primarily negative because you have credit card debt, then that's a big red flag. You need to act. Now.

Credit card debt is classified as "bad debt" because it has a high-interest rate (typically credit card interest rates are over 20%) and there is no appreciating asset associated with credit card debt.

The reason why I suggest you also determine your net worth is for this simple quote:

"To GROW your net worth, you first must KNOW your net worth."

Again, think about running (or walking, if you're me) that race blindfolded. You won't get anywhere. The same goes for your net worth.

At some point, especially if you're getting closer to retirement, you'll probably want to live a debt-free life. And if you have debt right now, you'll also probably want to find a roadmap to get rid of it.

Well, your net worth statement will at least give you an inventory of your current assets and liabilities. It can help create the foundation of your game plan to get rid of certain types of debt – like your credit card debt.

I will say one additional item:

Instead of tracking your net worth every single month (like you probably should do with your budget), a net worth statement only needs to be updated every quarter or so.

A net worth statement is like a snapshot of your current financial situation at a specific period in time. You don't need to consistently update it every day or every week.

Challenge #15: Become a Master Budgeter

As I mentioned earlier in this chapter, I want you to take out your calendar and schedule at least one hour of your time within the next seven days to go over your numbers.

Have some fun with it – pour yourself a glass of your favorite drink, eat some cheese or chocolate (or both!) while you go through your numbers.

First, let's start with your budget.

Then, I want you to put pen to paper:

1. Track how much you earn monthly.
2. Track how much you spend monthly.
3. Sort your purchases into the "needs," "wants," or "wishes" categories.
4. Compare your spending versus income with the rules of thumb in this chapter.

(Continued)

5. Cut at minimum one of your expenses this month, then cut another next month.
6. Consider downloading a budgeting app if you find you need the extra guidance.
7. Determine which changes need to be made in order to keep up with your new budget.

Once you start consciously tracking – and physically writing down these numbers – how much you earn versus how much you spend, you'll start to see where you can improve.

I'll give you a quick example

After using these budgeting rules of thumb, I helped a young professional couple cut down on over $600 per month (that's $7,200 per year) of spending. This couple took the "Ostrich" approach: They just stuck their head into the sand. They knew *something* was wrong, but they didn't want to know exactly *what* was off. When we finally sat down together, we quickly realized where this couples' weakness lay: they ate out almost every day.

Once we identified the culprit, it was just a matter of changing their habit to spend less and less on eating out (note how I didn't say completely *stop* eating out – that would not be a good option). While it did take some time to reduce their monthly expenses from $600 to about $100 on eating out, we did it. And their bank accounts (and credit cards) thanked them for it!

The first step you can take is reviewing your income and expense documents.

Your income information is likely found with:
- Your bank account statements.
- Your employer (Human Resources) pay stub.

Your expense information is likely found with:

- Your car bills.
- Your utility bills.
- Your mortgage statement.
- Your monthly credit card bills.
- Your monthly checking account statements.

Now that you know how to build your budget, let's shift gears.

The second piece to this challenge is building out your net worth statement.

If you've already built out your net worth statement in the past, then use this opportunity to update your net worth.

Here's what you should do:

- Open a new Excel document.
- Label one column "Assets" and one column "Liabilities."
- Now, start listing the assets you own along with their current market value.
- Next, start listing the liabilities you owe along with the current outstanding balance.

Now, you want to add up *all* of your assets under the "Assets" column. Next, add up all of your liabilities under the "Liabilities" column.

And the final step here is to subtract your total liabilities from your total assets.

So for example, if you have $50,000 of assets and $75,000 of liabilities, here's what you do:

$$\text{Net Worth} = 50{,}000 - 75{,}000$$

$$\text{Net Worth} = -25{,}000$$

(*Continued*)

In this example, the net worth is negative – but it's not far away from a $0 net worth.

Now it's your turn.

What's your net worth number?

If this chapter has taught you anything, it's to never look the other way or stick your head into the sand like an ostrich when it comes to money.

I completely understand that you may feel embarrassed or just plain nervous to see your spending numbers . . . but remember that you cannot win the race if you're blindfolded.

The moral is: start your life planning (aka budgeting) today.

Notes

1. Christie, Les. (3 Dec. 2014). The high cost of housing. [online]. CNN Money. https://money.cnn.com/2014/12/03/real_estate/housing-costs/ (accessed 2 July 2023).

2. Dickinson, Duo. (25 Jan. 2023). Column: Home size America. [online]. CT Insider. https://www.ctinsider.com/living/article/column-home-size-america-17738749.php#:~:text=The%20average%20new%20home%20in,of%202%2C500%20square%20feet%20today (accessed 3 July 2023).

3. 35% of Americans carry balances month to month, new study says (2023, January). Yahoo! Available at: https://www.yahoo.com/now/inflation-led-credit-card-debt-050100341.html?guccounter=1&guce_referrer=aHR0cHM6Ly93d3cuZ29vZ2xlLmNvbS8&guce_referrer_sig=AQAAALB16vqisMZ0a1nQ_TkRsjOBF8hzWeFTT7AYzAZkljbHhpJj_h31T0DPhrPc8NpJohiXEIS1XazB5K8rKyQSSFIvxHN-g5HpmQS996FASAeKt8X_u7ymmcHaEV8a306P1xFWEH-0PKt1uTZCGx4l7r8ceJEm5xZ9POphnEAUShVq#:~:text=Americans%20are%20leaning%20on%20credit,up%20from%2039%25%20last%20year (accessed: 02 September 2023).

4. Sommer, Constance. (23 Feb. 2023). States with most credit card debt. [online]. Bankrate. https://www.bankrate.com/finance/credit-cards/states-with-most-credit-card-debt/#education-level (accessed 5 July 2023).

Chapter 17
A Discussion about Debt

The easiest and fastest way to *not* become a millionaire is by getting into high-interest debt and NOT paying it off.

And simply put: if you are in debt, especially credit card debt, you are robbing your future self of opportunity.

Let me tell you a story of a young professional who came to me looking for advice many years ago.

She was in her late twenties and had been providing for herself since she was 16 years old. Unfortunately, growing up, this young professional had to learn about money the hard way, mostly through trial and error.

And sadly, no one had ever helped her understand the importance of staying away from credit card debt.

The year I met her, I discovered her income hovered around $50,000 and she held a fairly stable job position.

She told me that back in college, she was under the impression that credit cards are simply a tool for anyone to buy "stuff" and pay back the borrowed money whenever they wanted.

Oh, boy.

So, she went to college, applied (and got accepted) to a few credit cards . . . . And took out just under $30,000 in total credit card debt for . . . redecorating her student dormitory.

Ouch.

To be fair, she – and probably 99% of us – were not taught how high-interest debt can potentially damage your future.

In this particular person's case, she carried around $30,000 of credit card debt for five years, and just paid the minimum monthly payments.

And paying just the minimum monthly payments is a no-no.

Do you know why?

If you just make minimum payments, you're basically only paying what is owed to the credit card company (aka the interest).

Minimum monthly payments don't actually help you dent what is known as your principal balance (aka the amount that you actually owe — the amount that the interest payments are calculated on. In my example, the principal balance was $30,000).

And think about it, how do credit cards make money?

By charging you interest.

So it's only natural that the credit card monthly required minimum payments will only cover the interest portion. Never the principal balance – what you actually owe.

What's my point?

If you have credit card debt right now, then calculate how much you actually pay toward that credit card.

Is it just the monthly minimum required payment?

Or is it more than the minimum payment?

Let me give you an example:

- Let's say you used your credit cards to purchase fancy furniture for $100,000.
- The $100,000 is called your principal balance.
- Your annual credit card interest rate is 25%.

In this example, the 25% interest rate is based on the principal balance.

Let's say that for one year you just pay the minimum required payments (in other words, you're just paying the 25% interest rate). You don't even touch the principal balance (the original $100,000).

Do you know how much money in just *interest* you would be paying toward the credit card company?

You would be paying $25,000 *per year* in just interest! Not to mention, you'll still have to pay off the existing $100,000 balance.

If you want to decrease your interest payments, you will have to decrease your principal balance. Aggressively.

That means, you have to pay more than just the required minimum payment.

Let's say you want to pay off that $100,000 in five years.

Not only would you have to fork up that $100,000 but you would also have to pay 25% interest rate on your outstanding balance. That means you could be paying up to $167,503 for the privilege of borrowing $100,000.

That's not a good deal (at least not for you).

It's a great deal for credit card companies.

If you decide to pay off this $100,000 balance within three years instead of five years, you could save up to $30,000 in interest payments.

And, if you managed to pay off your $100,000 credit card debt within one year, you would only pay up to $12,616 in additional interest payments. That means you would save just under $55,000 in interest payments (vs. if you had waited to pay off your credit card debt in five years).

Hopefully these examples can show you the logic of *why* it is so important to stay away from high-interest debt – or why you *need to* pay off the high-interest debt ASAP.

The interest will eat away at your future wealth.

And billionaire investor Mark Cuban would agree with me as well. He is generally thought to have coined the following:

"If you use a credit card, you don't want to be rich."

Although I don't necessarily agree that all credit cards are bad (they do help you establish credit, which can help you buy a house, rent an apartment, and so on, and you can wisely use them to earn cashback, frequent flier miles, or merchandise), I do think that if you *carry* credit card debt and don't make a conscious effort to pay it off, *then* you are setting yourself up for failure.

So here's a very easy rule to remember, when you're thinking about buying something:

Don't borrow money you don't have.

It's really that simple.

If you don't have the cash to pay for it, then just don't buy it.

Now I know that it's much easier said than done. But this is where you have to start building that mental discipline (and consistency) to physically tell yourself to "STOP!" when you are thinking about swiping your credit card for an item or service that doesn't exactly enhance your life or isn't absolutely necessary.

And if there is one lesson you should learn from this chapter, it's this:

There are TWO types of debt: smart debt and bad debt.

Smart debt is debt held on appreciating assets like:

- Your house.
- Your education.
- Your own business.

Smart debt also typically has lower interest rates (generally less than 10%).

On the other hand, bad debt is what you want to get rid of ASAP.

Bad debt is debt held on depreciating assets and can include things like:

- Credit card debt.
- Payday loans.

Bad debt also typically has a very high interest rate, generally well over 20%.

Let's switch gears to the young professional woman at the beginning of this chapter. She had considerable bad debt, $30,000 of credit card debt.

So, what did she do to crush her debt fast?

We worked together to do what is known as a "balance transfer."

Using the balance transfer method, this young woman and I were able to crush her $30,000 of credit card debt in about 13 months. Not bad, if you're asking me.

Credit Card Balance Transfer

A balance transfer is a way to pay off your credit card debt where you move your existing credit card debt (with a high-interest rate) to a credit card (typically a new one) with a lower, often 0% interest rate so you decrease what you have to pay in interest on your credit card for a period of time.

It's important to note that the 0% interest rate typically is a teaser (aka intro) offer.

In other words, these 0% interest rates only last for a few months (typically between 12 to 21 months), which is *exactly* the time that you should be throwing every last penny that you have to pay off that credit card debt, when it is accruing 0% in interest.

One piece of advice I would give you:

Make sure to mark your calendars well in advance for when that introductory period is over. You want to know exactly when your interest rates will jump from 0% to the high credit card interest rates.

The last thing you want to do is pursue this method, not completely pay off your credit card debt balance, and then have the high-interest rates take you by surprise.

Here's a rough idea of how a balance transfer works:
- Research the best 0% intro rate credit cards.
- Apply to the best credit card with a 0% interest rate.
- Call customer service (I would call the customer service from my current credit card *and* from my new credit card) to verify how to transfer your balance from the credit card earning high interest to the new credit card with the 0% interest intro offer.
- Initiate the transfer.
- Start paying off your debt as fast as possible – before the 0% interest rate intro period ends.

Does a balance transfer work?

Typically, yes – but it depends on your personality (and this is where you have to be 100% honest with yourself).

Keep reading to understand what I mean:

When a balance transfer works	When a balance transfer DOESN'T work
You will commit to paying off your credit card debt.	You don't pay off the recently transferred credit card debt.
You won't rack up *more* debt on the new credit card you just applied for.	You actually use your new credit card to rack up *more* debt.

The WORST thing you can do is use your new 0% interest credit card as a means to enable your already bad spending habits.

If you believe you are someone who cannot curb your own spending habits, then DO NOT sign up to a 0% balance transfer card. It will only make things worse because this is a temporary fix.

There are some additional pros and cons of balance transfers that you should consider:

Balance Transfer Pros	Balance Transfer Cons
Potential consolidation (and simplification) of credit card payments	May pay for a balance transfer fee
Save money on interest	Low interest rate only lasts for a certain period
Could decrease your credit utilization ratio (which can increase your credit score)	You may not qualify for a balance transfer (you often will be required to maintain a good credit score to qualify for the new credit card)

While every credit card provider is different and sets forth differing requirements when signing up to a 0% balance transfer credit card, I will say that the average required credit score is typically 680+.

So, if you have a credit score of 680 or greater, you will typically qualify for a 0% balance transfer card.

Another item to remember when pursuing a 0% balance transfer is that the credit card companies will typically require a hard credit check in order to let you qualify for that new 0% interest credit card. The hard credit check will confirm whether you have the necessary minimum credit score to qualify for the card.

And typically speaking, a hard credit check may decrease your FICO score by a few points for several months before your FICO credit score increases again. So just be aware of this as well.

In the following I also list a few additional steps that you could consider to start paying off your credit card debt FAST:

- Acknowledge Your Debt
  - To decrease your debt level, first you have to accept the situation you are in and not ignore it.
- Consolidate Your Debt
  - If you have debt on multiple cards (as an example) with varying interest rates, you can elect to combine your debts into one debt. This option could lower interest rates and simplify your payments.
- Debt Avalanche Method
  - Pay off your debt by aggressively paying off the debt with the highest interest rate first, while making minimum payments on your other debts. From a numbers' perspective, the Debt Avalanche Method will make the most sense.
- Debt Snowball Method
  - Pay off the smallest debt first, while making minimum payments on your other debts. From an emotional and motivational standpoint, the Debt Snowball Method will make the most sense because seeing small progress can keep the momentum going.
- Earn More Money
  - Increase your income through side hustles or taking on extra work to pay off your debt faster.

- Cut the Cards
  - Stop using credit cards altogether and start paying with the cash that you have.
- Work with a Professional
  - It's OK to ask for help, and professionals can help you craft a customized debt repayment strategy to get you back on track.

In my opinion, the best way to paying off your debt – any debt – fast is by automating your payments.

When you automate your payments, you take away one extra decision in your life: committing to paying off your credit card debt.

When you automate, you make your life easier because automation is out of sight and out of mind.

That's why I try to automate everything in my life:

- Investments.
- Mortgage payments.
- Credit card payments.

Trust me, your bank accounts will thank me later.

How Fast Should I Pay Off My Mortgage?

So, we just spent a good chunk of time talking about credit card debt (which is the most common type of high-interest debt).

Let's talk about some other common debt types. Specifically, mortgage debt.

I've been asked so many times before about how fast one should pay off their mortgage debt.

If you own a home, then you likely have a mortgage ... which also likely means you have interest accruing on your mortgage balance.

Most mortgage interest rates range from 2.5% to 7% – some interest rates are lower and some are higher, and your rate really depends on your situation:

- Your credit score.
- Your home value.

- Your credit history.
- The current state of the economy.
- Your mortgage term (i.e., fixed, variable, etc.).
- Your home equity (how much of the house you own).

And a lot of other little things.

In fact, you might remember that in 2020 to 2022, interest rates in America had sunk to virtually all-time lows. At that time, you could have grabbed a 30-year fixed home mortgage for an interest rate below 3%!

Now, in 2023 and likely beyond, inflation hasn't made life too easy on us. Inflation caused the Federal Reserve to increase interest rates. And, in turn, that increase in interest rates made it much more expensive to borrow money. To give you a rough idea, rates have jumped from about 3% all the way up to 7% at one point!

Most people I speak to *hate* debt . . . they want to stay away from debt at all costs – and I don't blame them.

But . . . would paying off your house faster really make the *most* financial sense?

I think the answer really comes down to your personality, your financial situation, and your future goals (and since I don't know you, I can't say what's best for your situation).

But, I can draw from my personal experience.

When it may not make sense to pay off your home early:
- Your job is unstable (aka you could be fired tomorrow).
- You don't plan to live in your home for more than five years.
- Your home would be a large majority of your total net worth.
- You don't have enough cash to cover the additional payments to aggressively pay off your mortgage.
- You are young and want to take advantage of investing in the stock market to take advantage of compound interest.

These are some general examples of when it would not make sense to pay off your home mortgage early.

Personally, when I owned my home, I only made minimum payments toward my home mortgage because I love investing in the stock market.

And here was my thought process:

- In the stock market, you can earn a 7% to 9% average return.
- By paying off your home, you would get an average "return" of whatever your interest rate is (which could range anywhere from 3% to 7%).

But chances are, your mortgage interest rate will likely not be greater than the return you would be generating in the stock market.

I'd prefer to make the 7% to 9% return in the stock market versus the 3% "return" I'd be saving by paying off my mortgage early . . . .

Plus, I also didn't plan to live in my home forever.

But that's my personal situation, and that's why paying off my mortgage fast didn't make sense *for me.*

Here's when it may make sense to pay off your home early:
- You need the peace of mind to live debt free.
- You have extra cash to pay off your mortgage early.
- You are living in your "forever home" and don't plan to move.
- You will invest the money you "save" from paying off the mortgage early.
- Your home won't make up the majority of your net worth (i.e., your assets are already diversified, even after paying off your home).

I think it's important to note that you should be cautious about paying off your mortgage early, especially if your home would make up the majority of your net worth.

You don't necessarily want to be asset rich and cash poor.

And here's why:

I once knew a couple who were worth $1 million, but $900,000 of their net worth was tied up in their home's value . . . so literally 90% of their net worth was from an illiquid asset (aka you can't just withdraw money out of your home within a few hours – unlike in a savings account. That process often takes weeks, if not months).

Talk about lack of diversification.

So, while this couple was part of the two-comma club, they were still cash poor.

Just as you want to diversify the stocks within your investment portfolio (to decrease volatility and risk), you also want to diversify the *types* of assets you own (liquid assets like stocks vs. illiquid assets like homes, jewelry, paintings, etc.).

How Fast Should I Pay Off My Car?

I'm often asked this question as well.

There are a lot of opinions when it comes to cars, so again, I can't give you a black and white answer.

Here's how I personally manage my car debt:

- I buy a slightly used car (1 to 2 years old).
- I shop the marketplace for the best interest rate possible.
- Assuming I can obtain an interest rate for 3% or less, I finance my car and put my payments on auto-pay.

I am a car lover, but I *do not* see the value of buying an $80,000 car on a $50,000 salary.

That's financial suicide.

Cars are typically depreciating assets and spending hundreds of dollars a month on a car payment (plus don't forget paying for car insurance!) is just not worth it, to me.

The reason why I say cars are *typically* depreciating assets is because there are some cars out there that appreciate with time – but those cars are often collector cars or other very expensive cars that probably should not be used as your everyday means of transportation.

And right now, I'm talking about paying off the loan on your everyday transportation vehicle.

Below is a timeline of how brand-new cars tend to depreciate after you purchase them:[1]
- 1 minute after purchase
  - Your car would have lost about 9% to 11% of its value.
- 1 year after purchase
  - Your car would have lost about 20% of its value.

- 2 years after purchase
  - Your car would have lost about 32% of its value.
- 3 years after purchase
  - Your car would have lost about 42% of its value.
- 4 years after purchase
  - Your car would have lost about 50% of its value.
- 5 years after purchase
  - Your car would have lost about 60% of its value.

Of course, the depreciation assumes some of the following scenarios:

- You drive your car consistently.
- Your car becomes slightly used and/or damaged.
- You increase the mileage and usage of your car every year.

Although most of us do need a car to bring us from Point A to Point B, we don't need to spend a lot of money on an expensive car.

We can buy slightly used and safe cars for a reasonable price in an effort to avoid the massive up-front depreciation (which typically occurs between Minute 1 and Year 2 of buying a brand-new car).

As with all things in life, paying off your car loan early has some pros and cons.

Let's check them out:

Pros: Paying off your car loan early	Cons: Paying off your car loan early
You save money because you don't have to pay interest.	You may not be optimizing your money (aka you can earn higher returns if you invest in the stock market versus paying off your car).
You own the car.	You could owe prepayment penalties (call customer support first, to confirm).
You free up your cash flow.	While you are paying off your car loan early, you may restrict your cash flow.

For me personally, it does not make sense paying off my car early if I have a low interest rate (so that means typically below 7%) because I want to use my money in the stock market (and typically, the stock market has returns higher than the interest rates on a car loan).

Now, with that being said, I also bought one of the cheapest, used cars on the market. My car is now already 10 years old and I plan to keep my car for as long as possible (FYI – my car loan is paid off).

Make sure to do your own research and weigh the pros and cons of each option before you make a financial commitment.

Challenge #16: Pay Off High-Interest Debt First

For this challenge, take some time to think about how much debt you currently owe and the type of debt it is (aka high-interest debt or low-interest debt).

1. Write down how much debt you owe, the interest rate, and the balance.
2. Consider one of the ways to cut down high-interest debt (reread this chapter if necessary).
3. Start with and stick to your plan of action.

Remember this

When you hold high-interest debt like credit card debt, you really are robbing from your future self.

Bottom Line:

Start paying off your credit card debt ASAP. That's one of the BEST ways to move closer to financial freedom. Other, lower interest debt (like car debt or housing debt) is still important to pay off, but typically speaking you want to pay off your higher interest debt first, while still making minimum payments on your other debts.

Let's do it!

Note

1. Car depreciation: How much value will a new car lose? (8 May 2023). Ramsey Solutions. https://www.ramseysolutions.com/saving/car-depreciation (accessed 7 July 2023).

References

Acevedo, M.M., Angélica (2019). 25 Celebrities Who Were Rich and Famous before Losing All Their Money. [online]. *Business Insider.* https://www .businessinsider.com/rich-famous-celebrities-who-lost-all-their-money-2018-5#floyd-mayweather-jrs-nickname-is-money-for-never-losing-a-boxing-match-ironically-he-owed-money-to-the-irs-3 (accessed 1 July 2023).

Car Depreciation: How Much Value Will a New Car Lose? (8 May 2023). Ramsey Solutions. https://www.ramseysolutions.com/saving/car-depreciation (accessed 7 July 2023).

Causes of Divorce. (12 April 2023). Divorce.com Blog. https://divorce.com/blog/causes-of-divorce/ (accessed 4 July 2023).

Christie, Les. (3 Dec. 2014). The High Cost of Housing. [online]. CNN Money. https://money.cnn.com/2014/12/03/real_estate/housing-costs/ (accessed 2 July 2023).

Dickinson, Duo. (25 Jan. 2023). Column: Home Size America. [online]. CT Insider. https://www.ctinsider.com/living/article/column-home-size-america-17738749.php#:~:text=The%20average%20new%20home%20in,of%202%2C500%20square%20feet%20today (accessed 3 July 2023).

Doyle, Karen. (27 June 2019). 43% of Millennials Aren't Investing, Survey Finds. [online]. Yahoo! Video. https://www.yahoo.com/video/43-millennials-arent-investing-090000387.html#:~:text=Specifically%2C%2043%25%20of%20millennials%20aren,them%20accomplish%20their%20financial%20goals (accessed 10 July 2023).

Hinshaw, A. (5 Oct. 2020). *Seven Seconds to Make a First Impression –
Make it Count!* [online]. blog.thecenterforsalesstrategy.com. https://
blog.thecenterforsalesstrategy.com/seven-seconds-to-make-a-first-
impression#:~:text=Our%20brains%20make%20a%20thousand (accessed
2 July 2023).

Hodge, Scott. (15 June 2012). Who Are America's Millionaires? [online]. Tax
Foundation. https://taxfoundation.org/who-are-americas-millionaires/
(accessed 5 July 2023).

How Many Millionaires Actually Inherited Their Wealth? (2022). Ramsey
Solutions. https://www.ramseysolutions.com/retirement/how-many-
millionaires-actually-inherited-their-wealth (accessed 10 July 2023).

Jacobs, D.L. (20 March 2012). How A Serial Entrepreneur Built A $95 Mil-
lion Tax Free Roth IRA. [online]. *Forbes*. Available at: https://www.forbes
.com/sites/deborahljacobs/2012/03/20/how-facebook-
billionaires-dodge-mega-millions-in-taxes/?sh=32e184e658f3 (accessed 15
July 2023).

Kolmar, Chris. (17 Nov. 2022). Entrepreneur Statistics: The Latest Demographics and Trends. [online]. Zippia. https://www.zippia.com/advice/
entrepreneur-statistics/ (accessed 10 July 2023).

Leonhardt, M. (2020). Nearly 1 in 4 Millennials Report Having $100,000 or
More in Savings. [online]. CNBC. Available at: https://www.cnbc.com/
2020/01/30/nearly-1-in-4-millennials-report-having-100000-
or-more-in-savings.html#:~:text=In%20fact%2C%20almost%20half
%20(49 (accessed 15 July 2023).

McGrath, M. (2016). 63% of Americans Don't Have Enough Savings to
Cover a $500 Emergency. [online]. *Forbes*. https://www.forbes.com/sites/
maggiemcgrath/2016/01/06/63-of-americans-dont-have-enough-savings-
to-cover-a-500-emergency/?sh=3b370e874e0d (accessed 1 July 2023).

Most Successful Chimpanzee on Wall Street. (n.d.). Guinness World Records.
https://www.guinnessworldrecords.com/world-records/most-successful-
chimpanzee-on-wall-street (accessed 1 July 2023).

Passy, J. (21 Nov. 2021). Are You a Financial Cheater? Over 40% of Americans Say They've Deceived Their Partners about Money. [online]. Market
Watch. Available at: https://www.marketwatch.com/story/are-you-a-
financial-cheater-over-40-of-americans-say-theyve-deceived-
their-partners-about-money-11637346867 (accessed 5 July 2023).

Rising Stocks Create 300,000 New U.S. Millionaires. (2 Dec. 2021). Local
3 News. https://www.local3news.com/local-news/whats-trending/rising-
stocks-create-300-000-new-us-millionaires/article_93435602-a970-
5aad-a881-498d8a650051.html#:~:text=(CNBC)%20%2D%2D
%20The%20rising%20stock, time%20highs%20before%20the%20recession
(accessed 15 July 2023).

Sommer, Constance. (23 Feb. 2023). States with Most Credit Card Debt. [online]. Bankrate. https://www.bankrate.com/finance/credit-cards/states-with-most-credit-card-debt/#education-level (accessed 5 July 2023).

Stobierski, Tim. (19 Dec. 2022). Most Investors Wish They Got Started Sooner. [online]. Grow with Acorns. https://grow.acorns.com/most-investors-wish-they-got-started-sooner/#:~:text=Nearly%20 one%2Dthird%20(31%25),45%20years%20away%20from%20retirement (accessed 15 July 2023).

Tayal, Puja. (4 Aug. 2021) Monkey Beats Stock Market. [online]. Yahoo! Finance Canada. https://ca.finance.yahoo.com/news/monkey-beats-stock-market-172803113.html#:~:text=According%20to %20a%202012%20Forbes,large%20portion%20of%20the%20market (accessed 1 July 2023).

The Shape of Things to Come: Reverse Radical Recovery. (n.d.). Conference of State Bank Supervisors (CSBS). https://www.csbs.org/newsroom/ shape-things-come-reverse-radical-recovery (accessed 15 July 2023).

Unhappy Employees Statistics: Are Your Employees Secretly Unhappy? (21 March 2023). Gitnux. https://blog.gitnux.com/unhappy-employees-statistics/#:~:text=85%25%20of%20individuals%20worldwide% 20are%20unhappy%20in%20their%20jobs%2C%20according,and %20fulfilled%20in%20their%20roles (accessed 12 July 2023).

Williams, Geoff. (21 Dec. 2020). Cost Breakdown of a Divorce. [online]. *U.S. News & World Report* – Money. https://money.usnews.com/money/ personal-finance/family-finance/articles/cost-breakdown-of-a-divorce#:~:text=Average%20Cost%20of%20a%20Divorce& text=Still%2C%20if%20you%20want%20a%2C%20estate%20appraisers%20 and%20other%20experts (accessed 4 July 2023).

Wilkinson & Finkbeiner (2018). Divorce Statistics and Facts/What Affects Divorce Rates in the U.S.? [online]. Wilkinson & Finkbeiner, LLP. https:// www.wf-lawyers.com/divorce-statistics-and-facts/ (accessed 4 July 2023).

Index

Page numbers followed by *f* refer to figures.